STITCHERY
NEEDLEPOINT
APPLIQUE

AND

PATCHWORK

Also by Shirley Marein

OFF THE LOOM

STITCHERY NEEDLEPOINT APPLIQUE

AND

PATCHWORK

A COMPLETE GUIDE

Shirley Marein

Renderings by Eleanor Bello

Photographs by Alan Sweetman

STUDIO VISTA   LONDON

For Melissa and Peter

ACKNOWLEDGEMENTS

I wish to express thanks and an appreciation of all the artists who so generously contributed photographs of their work. Also to the many private collectors who allowed me to photograph their historical and contemporary examples, as well as my pleasure in the full and immediate response to my requests for supplementary material from the Dallas Museum of Fine Art, Dallas, Texas; the Shelburne Museum, Shelburne, Vermont, and the Victoria and Albert Museum, London, England.

Special thanks to Rosalie Adolf, Theda Sadock, Jan Silberstein, Celia Tobias, and Vesta Ward for help in preparing and finding examples of stitchery and needlepoint. And I am most grateful to my husband, Edmund Marein, for his patience, interest, and technical assistance.

During the exhilarating period of organization, the intense months of concentrated work and the tedious activity of tying up loose ends, my two assistants, Eleanor Bello and Alan Sweetman, have been steadfast and devoted, working tirelessly on the renderings and photography.

Designed by Shirley and Edmund Marein

Published in Great Britain by Studio Vista
Cassell and Collier Macmillan Publishers Limited
35 Red Lion Square, London WC1R 4SG
Copyright © Shirley Marein 1974
ISBN 0 289 70404.9

CONTENTS

FOREWORD

Stitchery has been in a period of fermentation for more than thirty years. The decorative fragile art of embroidery has expanded, changed course, burst boundaries, crossed borders, broken all rules, left the academy and emerged as a new form. Embroidery stitches have been adapted to the open-mesh canvas usually reserved for needlepoint. Traditional silk and cotton floss, linen thread, and woolen yarns have not been abandoned; they take their place alongside an expanding group of new fibers. Increased scale and added dimensions require compatible materials, and these have been found among things usually reserved for other purposes. Marine cable, jute, hemp and sisal twines, welting cores, raffia, leathers, metal, and plastic wire and tubing are all in use in surface knotting or in the medieval technique of couching.

Needlepoint, bargello, embroidery, patchwork, quilting, and appliqué all are alternatives in stitchery, just as a rainbow of colors on the palette represents an artist's range of choices. The four parts of this book provide a well-stocked file of stitchery ideas complete with the necessary tools for their implementation. Part I progresses from foundation stitchery forms of great simplicity to more complex composite stitches. Part II complements free stitchery on fabric with an explanation of needlepoint and bargello, two essentially structured forms of embroidery on canvas. For the reader who has acquired an increased understanding of the basic stitchery forms through practice and experimentation, Part III introduces many approaches to thoughtful design. Part IV deals with composite mediums such as patchwork, quilting, and appliqué. Use them singly, in combination, or all together as a way of expressing your feelings and ideas.

You have at your fingertips easily available materials and a working knowledge of various techniques. Tempered by an individual identity and an awareness of the importance of uniquely personal ideas, these can become the useful tools of free and spontaneous creation. Sometimes it is important to remember that the perfect lawn does not make a delightful garden; perfection at the expense of content can be very dull indeed.

Early nineteenth-century embroidery of a sailing ship by an American seaman, done in white and shades of blue wool on cotton. Collection Mr. and Mrs. Sydney Jacoff

8

EMBROIDERY AND CREWEL STITCHERY

PART I

An appetite for adornment, a desire to enrich and decorate surfaces, extends from primitive forest peoples to the most sophisticated city dwellers. The need for beauty is uniquely human. Further back in time than it is possible to trace, needles were fashioned from a splinter of bone, threaded with hair or dried grasses, and used for stitchery. The history of the fine art of embroidery parallels that of painting and possibly precedes the invention of weaving, for ancient burial mounds have uncovered fragments of intricately decorated animal skins. With no functional purpose and no utilitarian need for it, the art of embroidery nevertheless adds to the happiness and well-being of both craftsman and spectator. Adornment and enrichment of surface ranges from the embroidery of the smallest personal possession to the robes of kings; from sacred vestments for the church to creative exhibition hangings.

Our heritage of embroidery stitches over the centuries is a distillation of the results of experiment and use in every corner of the world. Works of almost unbelievable craftsmanship come from the Orient, the Middle East, and India. Pure gold, beaten tissue-thin and wrapped in a spiral around a silken thread,

Detail from a seventeenth-century Chinese panel embroidered in silk thread on green silk brocade. Collection Dr. and Mrs. Herbert Steinberg

9

Embroidered wool and cotton detail of a mantle from the Paracas Necropolis, Peru. 51½″ × 110″ 200–100 B.C. Dallas Museum of Fine Arts, Eugene and Margaret McDermott Fund, in memory of John O'Boyle.

Peruvian textile of the Paracas region. Detail of an embroidered figurative border. Little silhouette figures were cut from a foundation fabric, attached to a broad tape held taut between stretchers, and embroidered in a network of looped stitches. The looped stitches resemble knitting. As the figures have only a slight point of attachment to the foundation fabric, it is possible to work both sides. The three-dimensional headdresses and decorative fringes are made of a network of loops worked from a mesh chain.

was applied to silk twill fabrics in the Orient with extraordinary skill about the year 1000. Silk velvet was used as a ground for gold and silver embroideries during the thirteenth century in Europe. Gemstones, pearls, and semiprecious stones were used on royal cloaks with great skill and dazzling results. Egyptians, Persians, and Hebrews produced embroideries on cotton and linen. Wool fabrics embroidered with yarn are preserved from the Bronze Age in Scandinavia, in places as far south as Greece, and in areas as remote as Mongolia. The technical achievement of the Paracas Indian embroiderers of Peru has never been equaled. Straight stitch, the simplest of all stitches, and stem stitch, split stitch, and chain stitch are the basic stitches used in these embroideries and are still the most useful today. Probably chain stitch and its many variations are most universally widespread. Early civilizations used design elements representing things close to the lives of the people, sometimes realistic, but more often highly stylized.

Gold and silver couching on a velvet pillow cover, probably Turkish. Collection Mr. and Mrs. William Sadock

Cuff from a nineteenth-century Spanish costume. Raised and padded couched gold thread on velvet with gold needle-lace ruffle. Collection of the author

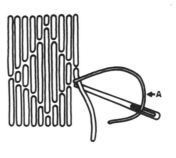

Medieval couching of gold and silver threads. The couching pattern is carried out on the surface of the foundation fabric with the aid of supplementary linen thread A.

A cross section showing the couched thread laid over the foundation material and held in place by the supplementary thread A.

The richly embroidered textiles of the Byzantine emperors were much admired and sometimes given as royal gifts, thus spreading knowledge of Eastern techniques to Spain, France, and other countries of western Europe. During the Middle Ages embroidery developed into a highly perfected art devoted to the sacred uses of the church. Men and women in monasteries and convents spent the long winter months designing and embroidering representations of the holy legends of both the Old and the New Testaments. Probably the most monumental work of art to survive, aside from ecclesiastical embroidery, is the Bayeux tapestry, preserved in the Musée de la Reine Mathilde in Bayeux, France. Approximately 320 feet long by 20 inches high, it utilizes 626 embroidered figures in action and about 730 animals and birds, and includes an inscription in letters an inch high running throughout. In addition it has a three-inch border of figures and animals at the top and bottom. It is the continuous tale of a progression of incidents during the Battle of Hastings, terminating in the Norman conquest of England in 1066. Spontaneous and spirited in concept, the embroidery is on linen in plied wool, using chain, stem, and split stitch, in addition to laid and couched work in earth colors. Uncertainty surrounds its actual production, but it is thought to have been embroidered some time within the twenty-year period after the conquest. The only other existing embroidery of appreciable size is the wall hanging in the Cathedral museum of Gerona, in Catalonian Spain. This eleventh-century Story of the Creation is

Section of the Bayeux tapestry depicting the Battle of Hastings. Possibly eleventh or twelfth century.

Man's nightcap, late sixteenth century. Linen embroidered with silver thread and edged with lace and spangles. Victoria and Albert Museum

Jacobean design incorporating carnations, thistles, acorns, and oak leaves in spiraling growth form.

a roundel with a square, charmingly naïve, on terra-cotta twill, embroidered with multicolored plied yarns and white linen thread in stem, chain, and satin stitch figures on a densely couched background.

At the close of the Middle Ages expanding foreign trade and spoils from India and China brought a change in the textile arts of western Europe, particularly England and the Lowlands. Many people of India and Asia regarded realistic representation of nature as a form of idolatry and devised highly stylized floral arabesque design elements. Much admired, these Indian fabrics, delicately painted or embroidered with gracefully spiraling trees and flowers, had a profound effect on the embroiderers of sixteenth-century England. Wealth and leisure during and after the opulent reign of Henry VIII, coupled with the rise of a mercantile class (and incidentally the invention and manufacture in England of the steel needle) brought about a revolutionary change in the artistic expression of the textile arts that has continued almost unabated until the present time.

Back of a woman's jacket, c. 1600, of silk embroidered with colored silk and silver thread and spangles. Victoria and Albert Museum

Although a prodigious embroiderer like Mary Queen of Scots employed her own designers, pattern books existed in the sixteenth and seventeenth centuries. Earliest patterns were printed in Germany, and later in Italy, France, and England. The most famous of these were Jacques Le Moyne's *La Clef des Champs* (1586), a guide to the flowers and insects of the countryside, Richard Shorleyker's *A Scholehouse for the Needle* (1624), and James Boler's *The Needles Excellency* (1640). The term Jacobean (a Latin derivation from James) applies to the stylistic period of the early seventeenth century when Mary Stuart's son James ascended the English throne on the death of Elizabeth I. Stuart emblems—the carnation, oak leaf, and acorn, in addition to thistles—soon intermingled with Elizabethan designs. The end of the seventeenth century united the Netherlands' William of Orange and Mary on the English throne, introducing strange new themes; for instance, the pineapple, a product of the Dutch West Indies, was soon to become a common theme in English and American art, architecture, textiles, and furniture design.

Intense interest in embroidering, highly prized as an activity that conferred status on the middle classes who previously had had no leisure time, expanded its usage and invited unusual experimentation in the seventeenth and eighteenth centuries. Variations on stitches, new techniques, exotic designs and fine fibers from all sources were eagerly adapted to both the whimsies and needs of Europeans. Embroidered upholstery fabric appeared on furniture. Stumpwork, named for the small wooden disks and molds used to raise and add dimension to flat embroidered surfaces, was a unique innovation. Wooden disks were covered with buttonhole stitch and other padding, dipped in wax, tinted, and painted. Pictures, as well as frames, casket tops, boxes, trays, and other containers, were worked in this fashion. Whitework, of white embroidery thread on white fabric; blackwork, of all black thread embroidered on white fabric; and drawnwork, cutwork, and needle-weaving increased a growing stitchery vocabulary.

A rich variety of embroidered textiles and embroidered rugs comes from the region of the Caucasus, a vast area extending from the Black Sea to southwest Russia and India. In addition to decorative coverings of all sizes for their possessions, the nomadic peoples of Turkmenistan, Bokhara, and Samarkand embroidered tent and portiere hangings. The designs are traditional and nonfigurative, with little change from generation to generation, minutely embroidered for the most part in red, ocher, and black. Indian embroidery is full, lavish, brilliant, and glittering with small mirrors. These circular disks are thin slivers of mica or silver-backed glass, held in place with a crisscrossing of straight stitches with buttonhole stitch worked over the straight stitches. Surrounding each shining disk is closely packed embroidery. Saffron-dyed yellow often predominates.

Early eighteenth-century Bokhara embroidery on linen. Collection of the author

Detail of Turkoman embroidery with Moslem inscription. Courtesy Artweave Textile Gallery

Nineteenth-century Bokhara tent-hanging embroidered on linen, part of young girl's dowry. Courtesy Artweave Textile Gallery

Door hanging from India, embroidered and decorated with small mirrors. Courtesy of Sona the Golden One

American nineteenth-century sampler worked with thread on a punched card. Collection Vivian Hale

Stamped sampler, a form of embroidery popular during the revival of American genre art in the 1940s. Worked by the author

The seventeenth century was also the age of the English colonization of the New World. America's first settlers, mostly drawn from the lower classes of society, brought with them only the barest essentials. Colonial families, far too busy seeking food and providing shelter and protection for survival, had little time for recreation. Embroidery requires resources and a certain amount of expendable time. As a result little remains from the earliest days in the colonies, and later work reflects the difficulty in obtaining and preparing materials. Clearing the land, growing flax (it takes almost a year and a half from planting to linen thread), and processing wool were arduous tasks. Much of the linen and wool was home-grown, hand-spun, vegetable-dyed, and hand-woven, although some fibers were imported. The need for economy and many other difficulties forced the American embroiderer to adopt simpler designs and more open techniques employing fewer stitches.

English sampler worked by Frances Whitworth in 1808. The illustration at the top honors William Wilberforce (1759–1833) and his support of the bill to abolish the slave trade passed by the British Parliament in 1807. Collection Mr. and Mrs. Sydney Jacoff

Sailing ship in raised and padded wools embroidered on a cotton backing by a nineteenth-century American seaman. Collection Mr. and Mrs. Eugene Goldberg

Every young girl was trained in the use of the needle at the time she was taught to read and write. The sampler is an embroidery copybook, a method of recording stitches or, as implied by its Latin forerunner, "exemplar," a model or example. The earliest known American samplers, much influenced in style by their English late-sixteenth-century counterparts, come from New England. Alphabets, Bible quotations, and morality verses contribute to the quaintness of old samplers. Family records, marriages, birthdays, and deaths appear more frequently on American samplers than on those of other countries. The interest in samplers disappeared before the turn of the twentieth century, with only a slight revival between 1930 and 1940, when Regionalism and the search for indigenous American art for a time renewed their popularity.

One of a pair of late nineteenth-century pictures commemorating Peace and Plenty, embroidered on delicately hand-painted silk. Collection Mr. and Mrs. Sydney Jacoff

Industrialization affected the mental and moral outlook of the people, as well as changed the economic and social factors of their daily lives. Unfortunately, when the great days of the whaling ships came to an end, the embroidering of seascapes by sailors to alleviate the boredom of long and tedious journeys also ceased. Mourning pictures were another unusual form that disappeared almost completely. These memorials, possibly prompted by the death of George Washington, were of weeping figures, often all in black, embroidered on silk. The last of the uniquely American forms to decline by the end of the nineteenth century were the thanksgiving testimonials to the goodness and fruitfulness of America, embroidered on silk backgrounds with delicately detailed areas painted in watercolors. Embroidered pictures, bed hangings, and decorated clothing represented beauty

Broderie Anglaise (English embroidery). White-on-white border detail from a large circular tablecloth. Collection Hanna Hale

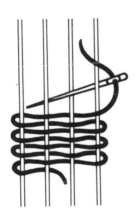

Needleweaving. Any number of foundation threads is suitable for needleweaving. Attach a supplementary thread to the material from edge to edge. Weave the supplementary thread back and forth, over and under, until the foundation threads are covered. Needleweaving can be worked over remaining threads on a drawn-thread background, on a fishnet background, or on spaced horizontal or vertical threads affixed to the edges of fabric or other supports.

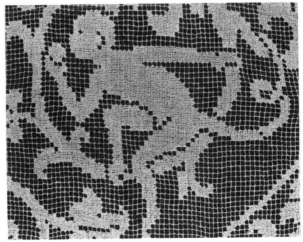

Linen needleweaving on knotted net linen background. Collection Hanna Hale

21

Needle-made lace similar in technique to the very early Italian reticella lace and to Venetian Point and consisting of buttonhole stitch, spider's webs, looped stitches, and needleweaving worked with a single thread over suspended bars. Collection of the author

Contemporary needleweaving on a fabric backing attached to a tambour ring. Gunnell Teitel, 1973

Needleweaving. Open spaces or slits in the weaving are made by working back and forth over a limited number of threads. Alternating patterns can be achieved by counting the threads and determining the depth of each unit of weaving. Random designs can be woven over odd or even numbers of threads.

and luxury in the early American home, adding gentility and graciousness to family living.

Intricate and delicate craftsmanship has always been much admired and is recognized by many people as a sign of worth. For centuries the nobility conferred a frothy distinction upon lacemaking, maintaining schools and workshops, even taxing the supply as a source of revenue and a way of ensuring exclusivity. Fashionable demand among Europeans as well as Americans created many derivations of the lacy look. Several age-old techniques popular until the close of the nineteenth century are of special interest. Not yet fully redefined, they have great potential for contemporary embroiderers. Among them are cutwork, also known as eyelet, broderie Anglaise, and Madeira work, or Richelieu work, named for Cardinal Richelieu. Eyelet embroidery consists of small repetitive designs, but Richelieu work is larger in form. In Richelieu work shapes of any kind and complexity are held in position, suspended in place by bars of thread strengthened with stitchery. The simplicity of needleweaving under and over foundation threads can be as academic as darning or as intriguing as a spider's web.

Although tastes and needs have changed with contemporary living, embroidery is as popular today as it has been in other periods. It is truly an art of the people, perpetuated from generation to generation.

Blue-jeans embroidery in red and white chain stitch. Carol Bello, 1973

Frog of appliqué and stem-stitch embroidery. Iris Lander, 1972

Pocket watch of appliqué and embroidery. Iris Lander, 1973

Polish peasant embroidered vest. Collection of the author

Threading the Needle: One or two strands of cotton floss may be moistened for easy threading; however, multiple strands of cotton or wool having uneven ends are more easily threaded by folding the ends back.

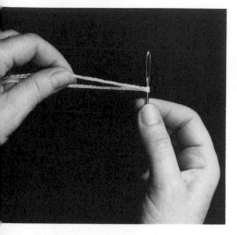

Fold several inches of yarn around the center of the needle.

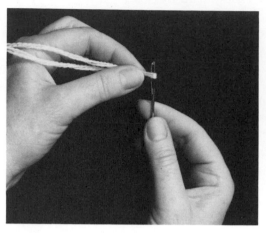

Holding yarn taut, move it up toward the top of the needle. Remove it from the needle.

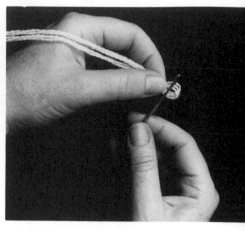

Push folded end of yarn through the eye of the needle. Draw through.

Hoops and stretchers: Round and oval embroidery hoops come in various sizes. Tambour hoops can be adjusted to accommodate many thicknesses. Artists' canvas stretchers are useful for squares and rectangles.

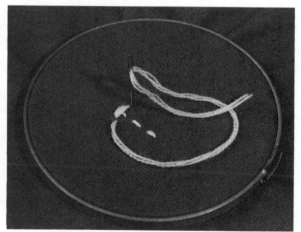

Starting and finishing thread: Avoid knotting by starting with a running stitch on the surface, to be covered later by the embroidery. Or run a new starting thread through the last few stitches on the reverse side. End in the same manner and clip the thread close. Very heavy strands such as those of rope or leather may be secured to the fabric with a small amount of white glue.

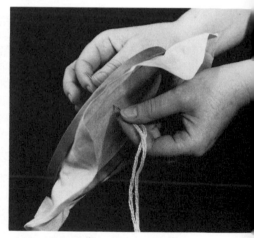

Embroidery: The finest and most accurate work is accomplished by working the needle up and down in single movements, holding the needle perpendicular to the fabric, rather than trying to go in and out in one motion.

MATERIALS
AND
STITCHES

THREADS AND FABRICS

The mutual suitability of fabric and thread is a prime consideration in stitchery. Thread must pull through the fabric easily, without abrasion, pilling, or puckering. Moderately open weaves are best. When the space produced by the angle of the vertical warp and horizontal weft threads in the canvas is just visible, the needle is easy to insert without splitting the woven threads. The threads in an open, even weave can be counted, and thus a greater regularity in the stitches may be achieved. Problems arise with softly spun, loosely plied thread when the fabric is very tightly woven. Soft gauze weaves may be difficult to manipulate, however, and will present problems in finishing. Linen is generally the most useful embroidery fabric, while the least desirable is burlap, a jute fiber. Test unusual fibers and synthetics. Fabrics composed of fiber blends, particularly those with percentages of polyester, tend to gather and pucker when sewn in layers. On the other hand, synthetic fibers do have great tensile strength. If home washing is to be a factor in care, wash a sample of the fabric before beginning the embroidery. An endless variety of fabrics is available. Your choice will depend upon the purpose of the embroidery, the size of the project, the color and texture in relation to your design. Purchase materials of good quality.

The desire to embroider is often stimulated by an attractive selection of embroidery threads in vibrant colors and intriguing textures. Threads vary greatly; some are more suited to certain stitches than others. The success of some stitches depends upon the choice of the correct thread. Smooth corded threads hold a knot better than soft slippery threads. Some woolen yarns are too fuzzy for sharply defined linear work; others, heavy and nubby, must be laid on the surface and affixed with a supplementary thread. Six-strand cotton embroidery floss is easily separated and can be used singly or in multiple strands. Three-strand Persian yarn can also be separated and used as desired. Both of these materials come in hundreds of tints and tones of many hues.

One- or two-ply thread is relatively slender, depending upon the fiber used in its composition. Six-ply yarn is usually heavy and suitable for rugs and wall hangings. Some fibers are loosely spun; others are highly twisted. A good tapestry yarn might be a four-ply, well-

CANVAS   AIDA CLOTH   LINEN AND RAYON   LINEN   DURABACK

WARP—

Vertical threads running down the canvas.

WEFT—

Horizontal threads running across the canvas.

twisted and smoothly finished. Some loosely twisted yarns will untwist during work; a few turns of the needle will retwist the yarn. However, many yarns will become too twisted during work, curling up and spiraling around themselves. In this case, allow the needle to dangle from the working surface and the thread will unwind by itself. Twenty-four inches is a good workable length. Change the position of the needle on the thread during work to prevent abrasion. Cut all threads with scissors or a blade. Never tear, bite, or break the thread, particularly from the surface of the embroidery.

NEEDLES AND SCISSORS

Needles, both blunt and sharp, are available in many sizes. There are also many special-purpose needles; particularly useful are curved upholsterers' needles and sailmakers' needles. One kind of needle will rarely be enough to complete a piece satisfactorily. The eye of the needle must comfortably accommodate the thickness of the thread. Crewel embroidery needles are of medium length and have long, slender eyes suitable for threading multiple strands. Darners are often preferable because the needle is longer. When using several colors, work with more than one needle to avoid the abrasive wear and breakage caused by repeated rethreading. Several needles threaded with the most used colors will save time and prove economical.

Large fabric shears and very small, sharp scissors with narrow, pointed blades are a part of basic stitchery equipment. To snip embroidery threads properly, the points of the scissors must close perfectly; therefore keep a special pair for embroidery and use it for nothing else. Tweezers are helpful in making changes and pulling out cut threads. There are special scis-

sors available for shearing rug piles. The blades lie parallel to the rug pile, while a raised handle makes the scissors easy to manuever.

HOOPS AND STRETCHERS

A taut and stretched fabric will ensure smooth, unpuckered work. Although very small areas can be worked without the aid of hoops and stretchers, it is preferable to use them. The secret of professional craftsmanship is a correctly stretched surface. Fabric is constructed on vertical warp threads that run parallel to the selvage. Weft threads cross the warp horizontally. Line the warp threads up parallel with the edges of the stretcher. The weft must cross the warp at right angles. Use embroidery hoops or stretcher strips. Stretchers and self-supporting hoops permit both hands to be free and help the fabric to retain its freshness because they reduce handling. Easiest to use are hoops. The tambour or round hoop and oval hoops come in a wide range of sizes. Large wooden tambour frames have adjustable screws on the outer frame, accommodating fabrics of any thickness. Artists' canvas stretchers are available in sizes increasing in inch gradations. Sizes more than 24″ tend to warp. Center supports are helpful, but large frames should be constructed of heavier weight lumber with angle irons at the corners for sturdiness.

Assembling Artists' Stretcher Strips

1. Apply glue to the slim protruding tabs and insert the tabs into the accommodating slots alongside each one. Gently hammer corners together. Be very sure opposite sides are parallel to each other and the corners at a ninety-degree angle before allowing the glue to dry. Round off sharp corners with sandpaper. Smooth away splinters.

2. Place background fabric right side down on the table. Put stretcher in center of fabric. Pull fabric up around frame. Place a thumbtack in center back of each side. Push thumbtack in halfway so that it can be easily removed for adjustment.

3. Use thumbtacks or an open stapler to secure fabric, tacking ½″ in from edges. Start at the center of each strip and tack toward the ends. Alternate from top to bottom and side to side, pulling fabric taut. Tack about an inch apart. Fold corners neatly and tack to back of frame.

EMBROIDERY HOOPS

1. Remove outer ring of hoop and place portion of fabric to be embroidered over inner ring.

2. Push outer ring down over fabric and inner ring. Working around the edges of the hoops, pull fabric taut.

3. Remove the hoops before putting the work away, so as to prevent unnecessary creases.

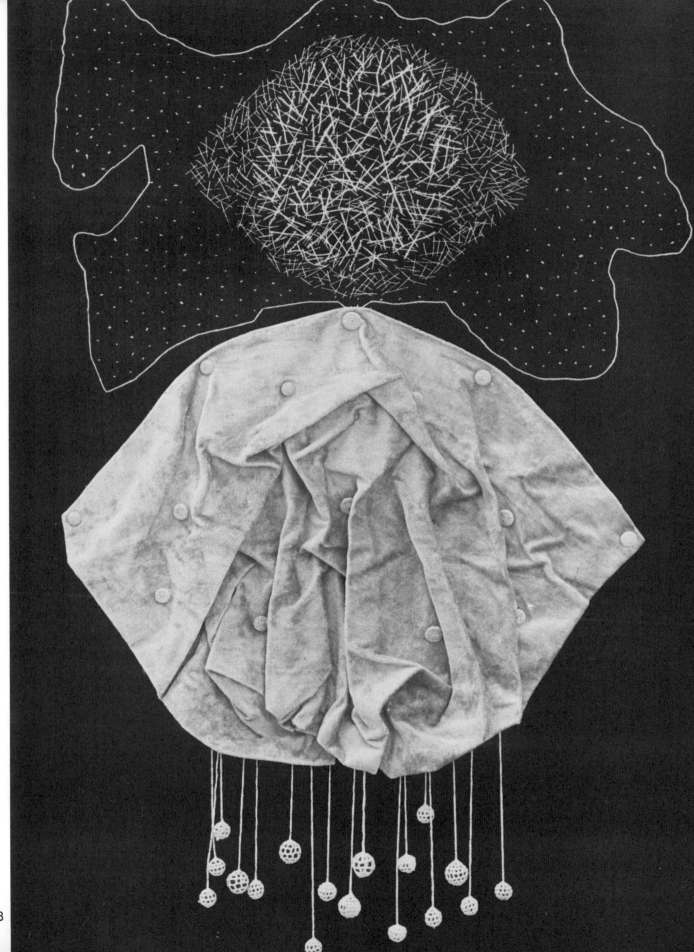

GLOSSARY

FLAT STITCHES

Straight surface stitches basic to the development of all other stitches.

CHAINED STITCHES

Complete circular loops linking one stitch to another. Large surfaces are thus rapidly covered with a minimum expenditure of thread on the underside.

KNOTTED STITCHES

Textural stitches employing knots in their construction.

LOOPED STITCHES

Curved flat stitches deviating from a direct course, made by looping the thread under the needle point before it is drawn through the fabric to complete the stitches.

COMPOSITE STITCHES

Two or more stitches used in conjunction with each other, such as those made by interlacing a supplementary thread through a running stitch.

These basic stitches are used in all types of embroidery. Any fiber that can be threaded through the eye of a needle, pulled through a background fabric with a tool such as a crochet hook, or affixed to a surface, is embroidery. Ornamentation is the sole function of embroidery. The term *crewel embroidery* usually refers to stitchery that has a certain density and is done with woolen yarn.

Each stitch is a development from another. Variations are as infinite as the names of the stitches. Names that have been in common usage over the years or are descriptive of their appearance are used in the text as identification.

FLAT STITCHES

STRAIGHT FLAT STITCH

Single stitches, spaced far apart or close together, regular in length or of varying lengths.

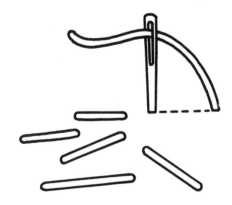

RUNNING STITCH

Stitches equal in size and spacing. Useful for outlining and as a foundation for composite stitches.

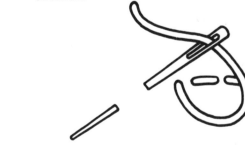

White and silver thread stitchery with eggshell velvet appliqué by Memphis Wood. Photo Larry Ebersole

BACK STITCH

For outlining and as a foundation stitch for other stitches, the back stitch is firmer and more solid than the running stitch. Bring the needle up at A, a short distance from the starting point. The first stitch goes back to the starting point at B. The next stitch begins at C, a short distance ahead of A, and goes back again to A.

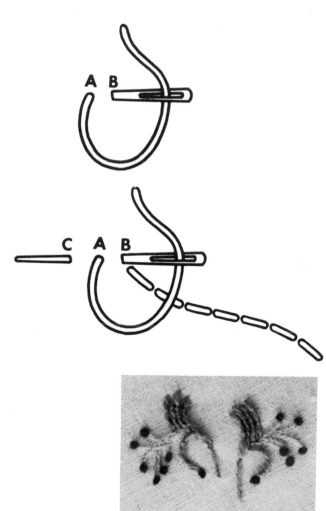

Lot's Wife *by Alma Lesch. Stitchery on burlap bag.* Collection Pat Newman

SATIN STITCH

Parallel straight stitches are set close together to cover a background surface completely. For a neat, firm line, pierce the fabric with the needle held vertically as it comes up and goes down. Do not overlap stitches. For a full effect, do not pull stitches too tightly. A closely spaced back stitch may be used as a guide by outlining the area to be covered. Satin stitch done over a back stitch outline produces a slightly raised effect.

Very long stitches look loose and have a tendency to snag. Break the surface to be covered by changing the direction of the stitches. Different directions enhance the play of light upon the stitches. Bands of satin stitches can be effectively shaded by using tonal values of a single color.

SURFACE SATIN STITCH

A surface satin stitch saves thread. Instead of carrying the thread across the back of the stitch, bring the needle point up very close to the finishing point of the last stitch.

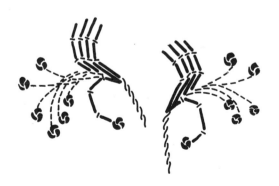

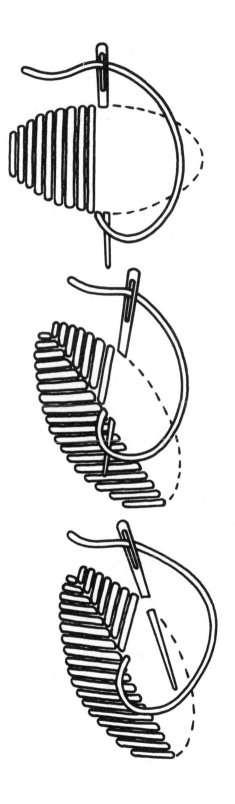

Water lily. White-on-white cotton floss embroidery in triple-padded satin stitch. The lily pad is filled with French knots. Courtesy Rosalie Adolf

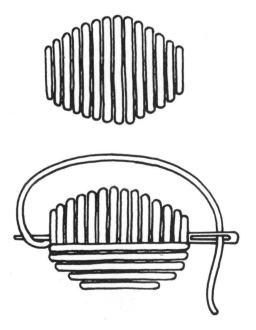

PADDED SATIN STITCH

For a raised and padded look, work a second row of satin stitches over the first row, but work in the opposite direction. An even higher, rounder look is achieved by adding a third layer of stitches. The directions of the rows should be planned so that the final row is stitched in the direction dictated by the design.

Opposite: Altar Panel by Memphis Wood, in the Unitarian Universalist Church of Jacksonville, Florida. Photo Larry Ebersole

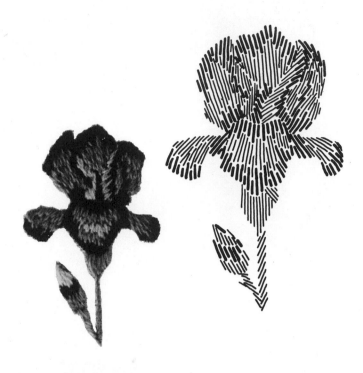

LONG AND SHORT STITCH

Similar to satin stitch, these stitches alternate in length on the first row, one long, one short. Make a distinctly noticeable difference in the length of the stitches. To fill in a designated form, keep one edge even and indent the other. Follow with long even-length satin stitches that meet the indented stitches of the previous row. A large background or undefined form may be worked outward from the center to the right and to the left. In an irregular area the broken line is softer and facilitates the blending of stitches.

Save time and thread on large-scale pieces by working from one stitch to the next adjacent stitch. Less thread will show on the reverse side. *Brick stitch shading* is named for the regularity of tonal shading imparted by the alternating technique. Do the first row in long and short stitches and work the subsequent rows in even satin stitches in the longer stitch length used in the first row.

Carnation. Seventeenth-century embroidery in long and short stitch and stem, herringbone, and satin stitch with laidwork and couched work in silk thread on linen. Victoria and Albert Museum

Iris embroidered on white satin with parts of the design raised by padding. Victoria and Albert Museum

35

Left: *Embroidered Chinese silk panels inset on an evening purse.* Collection of the author

Below: *Detail of stitchery in red, oranges, blues, and greens on Duraback by Shirley Marein.*

Opposite, above: *White-on-white cotton floss embroidery of the late nineteenth century worked in double-padded satin stitch, back stitch, couching, and buttonhole stitch with a drawn-thread background behind the figure.* Courtesy Jan Silberstein

Opposite, below: Moon Man *by Memphis Wood.* Collection Joanne Waites. Photo Larry Ebersole

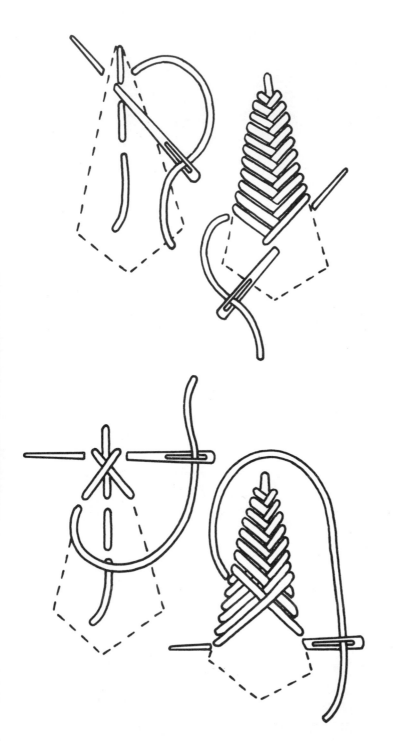

Tulip embroidered with wool on cotton and linen twill. Victoria and Albert Museum

FISHBONE STITCH

More closely resembling a Christmas tree than fish vertebrae, the fishbone stitch is started with a few running stitches beginning halfway down and ending at the topmost point of the tree. Bring the needle up on the right margin. With a deep slant, insert the needle on the far side of the running stitch, bringing it out on the left margin. For the next stitch insert the needle to the right of the center running stitch, bringing it out on the right margin. The needle always points to the outside from the center, where each stitch crosses the other, over the running stitch. An *open fishbone stitch* is worked in the same manner, but with the veins or ribs spaced an equal distance apart rather than close together.

RAISED FISHBONE STITCH

Start the raised fishbone stitch with a running stitch reaching to the topmost point. Make a deep cross over the top stitch and bring the needle up on the left-hand margin of the form, below the left leg of the cross. Insert the needle from right to left under the upper section of the cross. Cross down and insert the needle from right to left. The needle is always inserted horizontally, from margin to margin.

Early sixteenth-century embroidery of a moss rose in silk and silver-gilt thread on a linen ground appliquéd to dark blue velvet. Victoria and Albert Museum

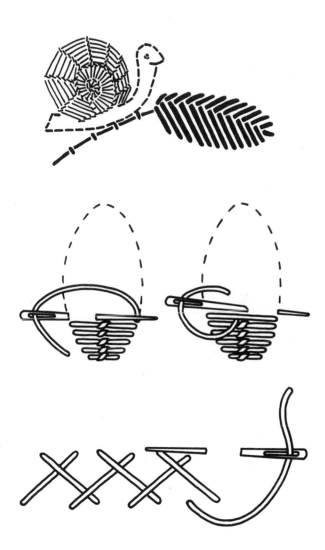

RUMANIAN STITCH

A practical filling stitch, opaque and slightly textured, adaptable to a variety of lengths and characterized by a long straight or oblique stitch tied down with a shorter stitch across the center. Bring the needle up on the left-hand side of the form. Insert it on the right-hand side. Hold the thread below the needle. With the needle pointing toward the left, bring it up at right of center and draw it through. Bring the thread over the long straight stitch and reinsert it at left of center, making a small short stitch across the laid straight stitch.

HERRINGBONE STITCH

Run stitches along parallel guidelines, either imaginary or drawn with a pencil, picking up only a small amount of the backing fabric. Start from the left, working from left to right. The underside of the work shows little thread, so it is especially adapted to transparent fabric. When closely worked without spaces between stitches, the herringbone stitch looks like a variation of the satin stitch. It is often referred to as the *double back stitch.*

Architectural Geometric *by Pauline Shapiro. Cross-stitch on fine cotton mesh, embroidered with cotton floss.*

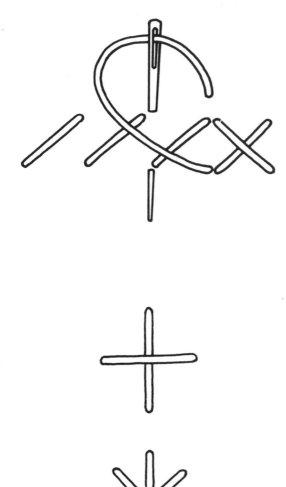

CROSS-STITCH

The time-honored, versatile cross-stitch, stand-by of the sampler, is precisely worked when it is done on loosely woven fabric. The horizontal and vertical threads of the fabric must be counted to assure even size and accurate shape in the stitches. Expert cross-stitch embroiderers of the Ukraine and the Balkan States baste a marked open-mesh scrim, similar in weave to penelope canvas and available in several sizes, to any desired background fabric. The cross-stitches are then worked over the mesh. The mesh is cut in several places, and its warp and weft threads are drawn out from under the cross-stitches, using a tweezer for especially small work. This leaves the background fabric clean and unmarked. Start with a row of slanted stitches to form the first half of each cross-stitch. Work back over these stitches to complete the cross. Cross-stitches may be worked individually and in any direction, but it is most important that all cross in the same direction, for a neat, even appearance. However, cross-stitches may also be placed with a certain abandon in improvised designs.

STAR STITCH

Work an upright cross, then make a diagonal cross-stitch over this to form a star. There are many kinds of cross-stitches and star stitches and a variety of different names for them, specifically for those worked on canvas. The many variations of cross-stitch and star stitch are best suited to canvas work.

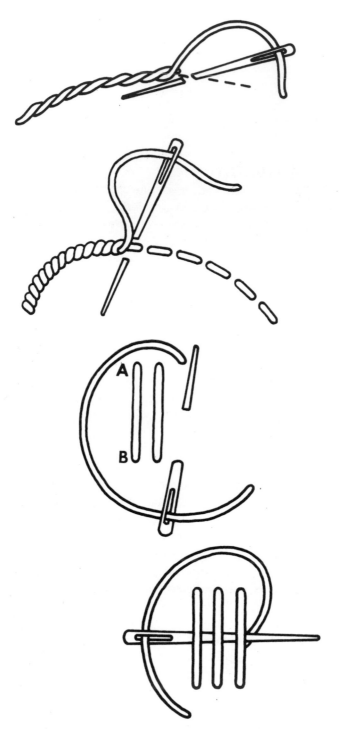

STEM STITCH

Often called *outline stitch* or *crewel stitch,* this stitch is found on the earliest known embroideries. The Bayeux tapestry is in great part composed of stem stitches. As you work, hold the thread either to the left or the right of the needle. Working from left to right, bring the needle up at the end of the line to be covered. Insert the needle point a short distance ahead, bringing the point out halfway between the place of insertion and the starting point.

OVERCAST STEM STITCH

A stronger line, raised for emphasis, can be achieved by working small, close stem stitches over and around a row of back stitches.

SHEAF STITCH

Construct three vertical straight stitches, spaced an equal distance apart. Bring the needle up beneath the last stitch, a bit above center. Wrap the thread around the group of three straight stitches once or twice without picking up any of the background fabric. Draw them together gently. Insert the needle beneath the stitch on the opposite side.

Der Unteilbare Rock *by Lissy Funk, 1960. Embroidered tapestry.*

Panel III from triptych Man *by Miriam Sachs. Stitchery tapestry on canvas in wools, silks, raffia, and metallic threads.*

SEED STITCH

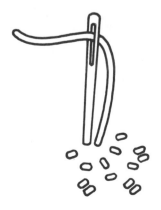

These very small stitches, taken in any direction, can be used as a light filling for design areas or as a method of adding texture to a smooth surface. Keep the stitches equal in length, placed at random. Very tiny stitches are best doubled, one stitch directly over another, or placed in groups of two stitches, randomly spaced.

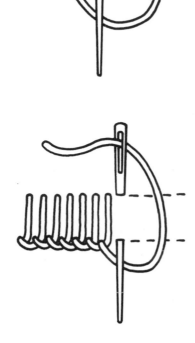

LOOPED STITCHES

BUTTONHOLE STITCH

The buttonhole stitch is the basis of all looped stitches. When used as an edging, it is called *blanket stitch,* and it serves decoratively in various adaptations. Work from left to right, starting the stitch from the bottom at A. Hold the yarn down with your thumb and bring the needle and thread around to the right, inserting at B, and at a desired distance above A. Bring the point out over the loop very close to A for a closed buttonhole stitch, or farther away for the *open buttonhole stitch.* Try a *long and short open buttonhole stitch.* Turn the work on the side, varying the length and spacing of the stitches. Join the tops of every two stitches by putting the needle in at the same spot at B. Or slant one of a pair of stitches to the right at B, and cross the second stitch over the first by slanting it to the left.

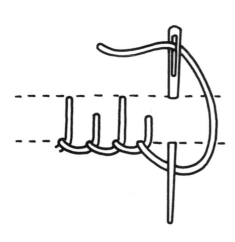

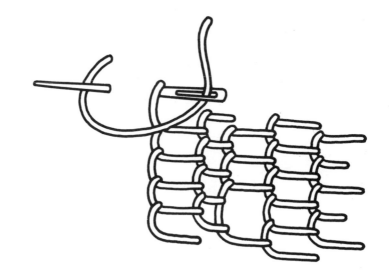

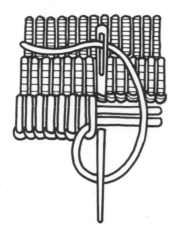

SHADED BUTTONHOLE STITCH

Shading the buttonhole stitch can be accomplished in a number of ways. If the background is to be solidly filled, work each new row of buttonhole stitches over the heading of the previous row. An interesting color variation is made by laying horizontal straight stitches of one color across an area, then embroidering over them with buttonhole stitches of another color.

DETACHED BUTTONHOLE STITCH

Detached buttonhole stitch is entirely free from the ground fabric. Work the buttonhole stitch over one or two straight stitches laid across the desired area. Complete a single row or continue to any length. The stitches on the diagram are spaced for clarity. In practice, they are formed closer together. Work succeeding rows into the bottom of the last row, stitching first and last stitches through ground fabric as shown, maintaining the width. The width can be increased or decreased with practice.

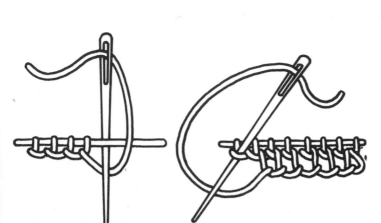

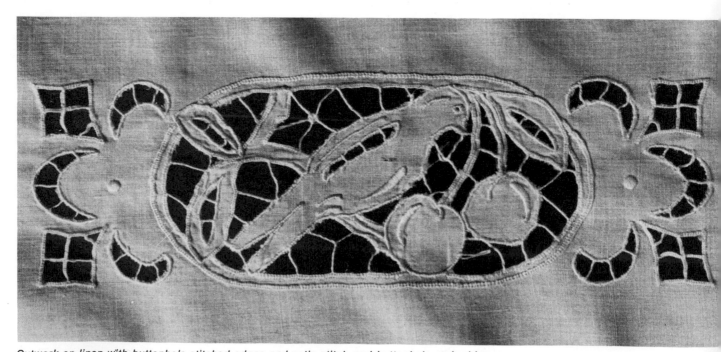

Cutwork on linen with buttonhole-stitched edges and satin-stitch and buttonhole embroidery. Note the minimal points of suspension on the birds and cherries. Courtesy Rosalie Adolf

MADEIRA WORK

Broderie Anglaise, now commonly known as Madeira work, and *Richelieu work* should be planned and drawn on the background fabric. There is a small distinction between the two forms. Traditional Madeira is finished with smooth, long-wearing satin stitch, whereas Richelieu work is often done in buttonhole stitch with small looped picots breaking the edges at intervals. Both are a form of open cutwork, and contemporary embroiderers often combine satin stitch and buttonhole stitch on one piece. The designs to be cut out are outlined with a small close running stitch, picking up the least amount of material possible in order to keep most of the thread on the surface. Cut the fabric out with scissors or a sharp blade, but leave at least ¼″ or more inside the running stitch outline, cutting away superfluous fabric. Roll the fabric back between index finger and thumb, stopping at the running stitch. Overcast the edges with satin stitches set close together without overlapping. In order to suspend fabric forms held with bars within the openings, lay several foundation threads from surface to surface, attaching threads to the material at each edge. Cover foundation threads with buttonhole stitch or, if double threads are used, with needleweaving.

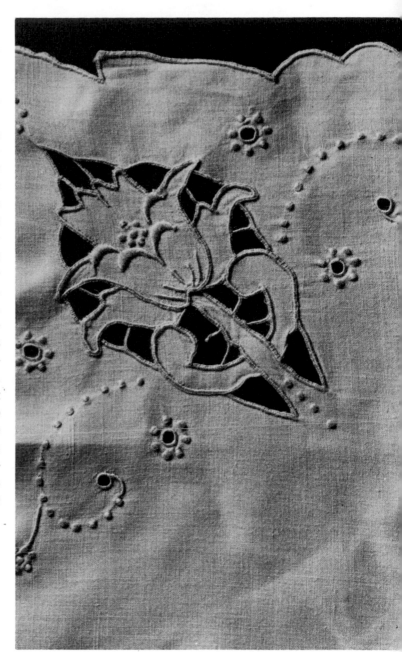

Madeira cutwork on linen with satin-stitch embroidery and buttonhole-stitched edges. Courtesy Rosalie Adolf

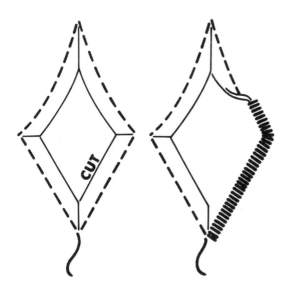

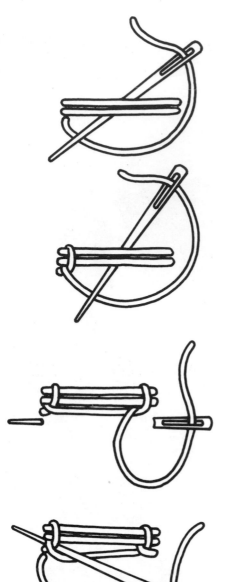

LADDER STITCH

Most handsome of the looped stitches, the ladder stitch can be constructed in varying widths. Start at the top left with two satin stitches, with the thread emerging on the left. Loop the needle and thread through the left side of the two satin stitches and draw the needle on through without picking up any background fabric. Bring the thread to the right and loop it through the right side of the two satin stitches. Now pass the needle horizontally back through the fabric to the left as shown in the third drawing. With the needle pointed to the left, loop it through the corner cross of the single stitch above. Draw the needle and thread through, bring it to the right, and loop it through the corner cross of the single stitch from the outside. (The needle always points to the left each time a single stitch at the left or right corner is looped.) After the initial double satin stitch at the top, each single ladder stitch may be closely or openly spaced, graduated in width, or stitched in undulating lines.

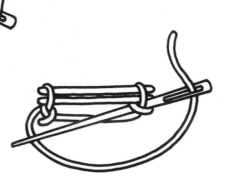

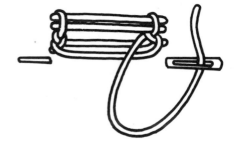

Opposite: The Nature of Materials *by* ***Alma Lesch.*** *Hooking, knotting, and stitchery on linen and burlap.* Collection Dr. and Mrs. Thom Colley

The Annual *by Alma Lesch. Natural fibers and white thread stitchery on
burlap seed bag. Collection J. B. Speed Art Museum, Louisville, Kentucky*

CRETAN STITCH

Cretan stitch not only provides wonderful coverage for wide spaces; it adapts easily to graduated or undulating forms. Stitches can descend closely or be openly spaced. Place several widely spaced rows side by side, dovetailing the stitches. Add variations by changing the quantity of material picked up on the needle, as shown in the second drawing. If the needle is inserted diagonally, the appearance of the cretan stitch changes to resemble the *Vandyke stitch.*

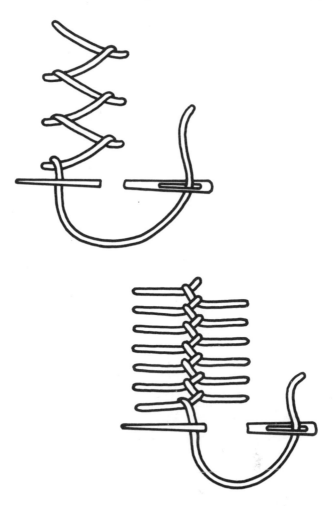

VANDYKE STITCH

Vandyke is essentially a linear stitch with a sinewy braid down the center. Make a deep, wide-legged cross as shown. Without picking up the background material, loop the thread under the intersection of the cross. Uneven tension tends to pull the center braid to one side. When this happens, picking up a bit of the background fabric behind the cross is helpful. Shorter crosses will produce a more prominent braided effect down the center.

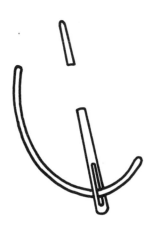

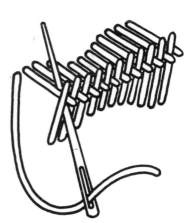

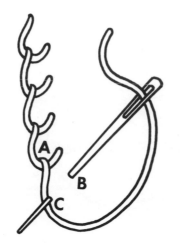

FEATHER STITCH

Bring the thread through from the back at A. Insert the needle at B, looping the thread under the point at C, where the needle emerges directly under A. A single feather stitch can be embroidered by working the first step from A to B to C repeatedly. Alternate the stitch from side to side by inserting the needle at B on the right side, completing a single stitch, then reinserting the needle at D on the left side. The feather stitch curves and turns easily to make leaves and tendrils. The *double feather stitch* produces a zigzag by alternating two complete stitches to the right with two to the left.

FLY STITCH

A single unit of the feather stitch terminated at the bottom with a short or long straight stitch is sometimes referred to as the *Y stitch* or *fly stitch*.

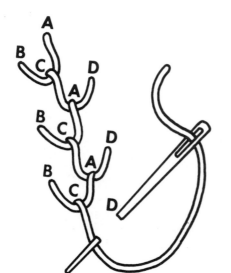

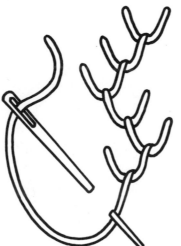

CEYLON STITCH

This series of loops worked across a straight stitch closely resembles knitting and could be used to repair a worn section of a sweater. Make a straight stitch from A to B, bringing the needle out at C to start the loops. After the final loop on the right, insert the needle at D. Do not pull too tightly. Bring the needle and thread across the back of the fabric, the point emerging again on the left at E. Start the series of linked loops again from left to right, working around the loops of the previous row, without going through the fabric. This stitch is extremely interesting on large-scale hangings; the overlay creates an effect of extra dimension. On very wide surfaces do not pass the thread behind the fabric; end each row of loops and start anew on the left with looping thread or cord.

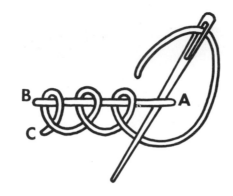

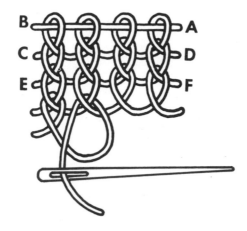

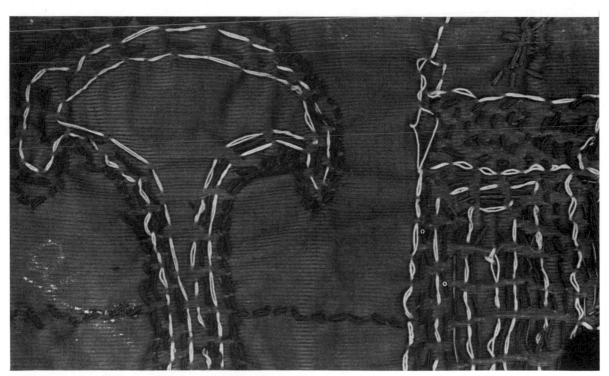

Landscape by an eight-year-old child in a special ungraded class in the Chicago public school system.

54   *Contemporary rug from area south of Baghdad, Iraq. Chain stitching in wool on hand-woven fabric in red, pinks, and oranges.* Collection Michael Silbert

CHAINED STITCHES

DETACHED CHAIN STITCH

Petal or Lazy Daisy Stitch

This is the basis of all chained stitches, used universally by the early Chinese, the East Indians, the medieval Europeans, and now by contemporary embroiderers. Each stitch forms a complete loop evenly covering a relatively large surface area with little thread showing on the reverse side. Bring the needle up through the fabric. Hold the thread down and to one side with your thumb. Bring a loop toward the right. Insert the needle at A. Make a straight stitch across the back, bringing the needle up again at B, over the looped thread. Tie the loop in place with a small straight stitch.

Details of rug on opposite page.

55

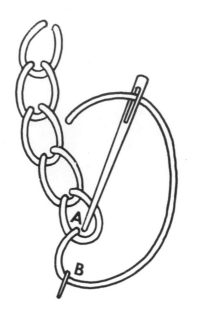

CHAIN STITCH

Make a loop as for the detached chain stitch. Inserting the needle either very close to A or in the same hole at A, bring the point out straight ahead at B, over the loop. Repeat, inserting the needle very close to or in the hole at B, inside the previous loop. Stitches can be any length, but an advance of about ⅛″ produces 3 chain stitches, each ½″ long, an ideally textured filling stitch when rows are close to each other. Small stitches are necessary in executing a graceful curve or spiral. The *zigzag chain stitch* is worked in the same manner as the regular chain stitch. Make the zigzag by inserting the needle at A, bringing the point out at a sharp angle to the left for the first chain and at a sharp angle to the right for the next chain. Alternate each chain. *Checkered chain stitches* are made by threading the needle with two separate strands of contrasting color. Begin in the same manner as for the regular chain stitch. When the needle is in position to pull through, pull it through only one color. With the thumb holding both colors to one side, place the needle again and alternate the color over the needle. Continue alternating colors for each stitch, or work two or three stitches of one color in succession, then two or three of the alternate color.

Winter Light *by Terrin Levitt. White on white with stitchery and appliqué.*

TWISTED CHAIN STITCH

Try the twisted chain for an interesting cabled rope effect that holds and follows a line most satisfactorily. To start, bring the needle through the fabric. Hold the thread down toward the left with the thumb, bringing the remainder of the thread to the right. Insert the needle in the fabric just below the starting point and a little to the left of the thread. Bring it through a little lower and on a slant to the right of the thread, in the center of the loop. Draw the needle through to complete the stitch. Use two or more strands for a raised effect. Experiment with this stitch, slanting the needle at different angles to change its appearance.

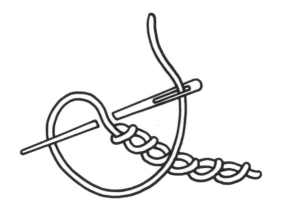

Denim shirt embroidered in multicolored cotton floss by Carol Bello.

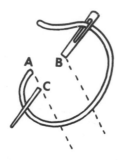

OPEN CHAIN STITCH

Made narrow or wide, close or open in spacing, the handsome open chain is adaptable to contemporary stitchery. Bring the thread through on the left-hand side. Hold the thread down and to the left. Insert the needle on the right at B, bringing it up on the left at C, over the loop of thread. Before drawing it up completely, insert the needle at D, loosely stretching the loop across the desired span.

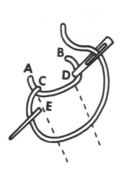

Stitchery in Blues and Greens *by Mariska Karasz (1958), an early creative force in contemporary stitchery.* Courtesy Bertha Schaefer Gallery

Detail of Stitchery in Blues and Greens

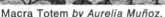
Macra Totem *by Aurelia Muñoz.*

ROSETTE CHAIN STITCH

The Rosette chain stitch makes a pretty border edging and works easily around circular shapes. Bring the thread up at the right-hand upper end of the section to be embroidered. Move the thread across to the left, holding it down loosely with the left thumb. Take the thread around in a loop to the right, inserting the needle again at B. Bring the needle point up at the desired length of the stitch, over the loop at C. Hold the loop loosely in place as you draw the thread through and around to the right, passing it under the thread coming from the previous stitch without picking up any of the fabric. Handle this stitch gently; drawn up too quickly and tightly it pulls out of shape. Use at least two strands of three-strand Persian yarn or any other coarse, twisted, or polished thread for a firm, well-defined stitch; it cannot be done with fine, slippery thread.

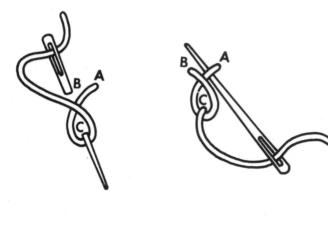

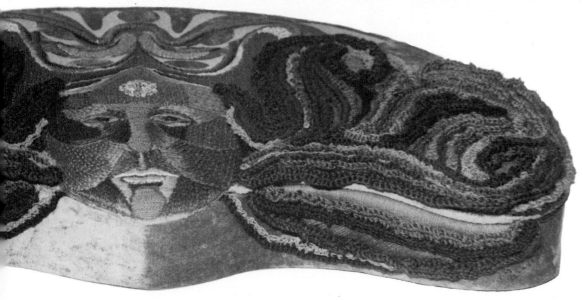

Pandora's Box *by Norma Minkowitz. Stitchery, crochet, and beading stretched over a frame.* Collection Mrs. Kenneth Hall. Photo K. Y. Fung

SPLIT STITCH

Certain stitches have come down to us from the Middle Ages and from early Chinese embroidery, in which the work was executed in silk on silk fabric that was stretched on a frame rather than hand-held. Split stitch used in this manner makes a smooth, flat, and very controlled line or solid filling even when it is shaded. It can be worked in a hoop by bringing the needle up through the fabric and then down again in two separate motions. When the thread is below the fabric, hold the thread taut between the fingers before stabbing the needle upward to split the strands of the previous stitch. Although the needle usually pierces the working thread in the center of a short straight stitch, the process can be applied to making longer stitches by piercing the straight stitch closer to its end, with the same stabilizing effect. Bring the thread through the fabric and make a straight stitch about ¼″ long. Bring the needle up from the back of the fabric, splitting the yarn with the needle. Advance to the next stitch.

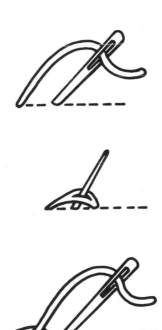

Skimmer by Ann Arink. Split stitch and straight stitch embroidery in muted colors.

Homage to Jerome Bosch *by Aurelia Muñoz.* Collection Provinciehuis, 's-Hertogenbosch, Noord-Brabant, The Netherlands

KNOTTED STITCHES

FRENCH KNOTS

Keep the fabric taut, preferably in a hoop or on stretchers. Bring the needle up at A. With the thumb and index finger of your other hand, wind the thread twice around the needle. A single twist around the needle will make a delicate knot on a fine fabric; two or as many as five twists work well on coarser fabrics. Hold the thread taut. Insert the needle point very close to A but not in the same hole. With the needle halfway down, pull the thread firmly to one side and slide the knot down to the surface of the fabric. With the knot held tightly against the fabric, push the needle slowly through to the underside, pulling the thread down through the center of the knot.

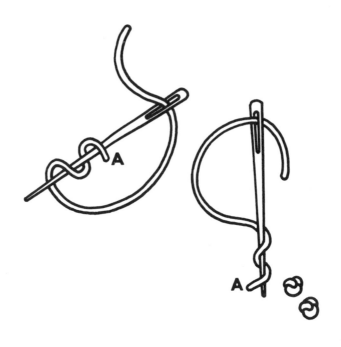

FRENCH KNOT VARIATION

Rather than a single dot effect, this slight variation adds a linear quality to the French knot. Bring the needle up at A. Wind the yarn twice around the needle. Hold the thread taut. Insert the needle point at B and slide the twisted thread down. B may be any distance from A. The distance is determined to some extent by the weight of the fiber used. Complete the stitch as described for French knots.

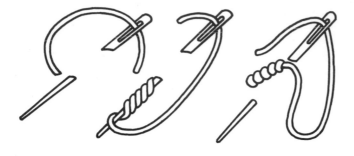

BULLION KNOTS

Bring the thread up through the fabric. Insert the needle back the length of the stitch required, bringing the point out in the same spot that the thread first emerged from the backing fabric. Do not draw the needle through. Wind the thread around the point of the needle as many times as needed to equal the length of the required stitch. Place the thumb on the twists to hold them back; draw the needle and thread through the fabric and the twists. Pull the needle and twisted threads back to the right and tighten the working thread until the twist-wrapped thread is in position. Insert the needle back down through the fabric opposite the starting point to complete the stitch.

CORAL STITCH

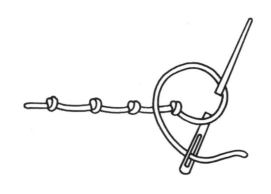

Textured and decorative, the coral stitch is particularly suitable for borders that have straight and curved lines. It is frequently used in closely formed lines to make a dimensional surface filling. Bring the thread up at the start of the line to be covered. Hold the thread down with your thumb, along the line. Make a tiny slanting stitch under the thread the desired distance along the line. With the thread under the needle point, draw the needle along the line. With the thread under the needle point, draw the needle through. There are several variations on the coral stitch. It works well in a zigzag.

DOUBLE KNOT CORAL STITCH

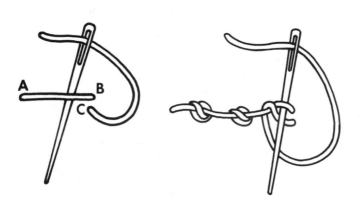

Slightly raised off the surface and more impressive than the coral stitch is the double knot coral stitch. Bring the needle up at the start of the line, at A. Advance the desired distance horizontally, then pierce the fabric at B, making a small downward stitch, while slanting the needle slightly to the left, to C. Draw the thread through. Loop the thread over the horizontal straight stitch without picking up any of the background fabric. The loop will leave a small space at the right side of the straight stitch. Bring another loop to the right, holding the loop down with the thumb. Pass the needle behind the small space at the right without picking up any fabric. Draw the needle through over the loop of thread to complete the knot.

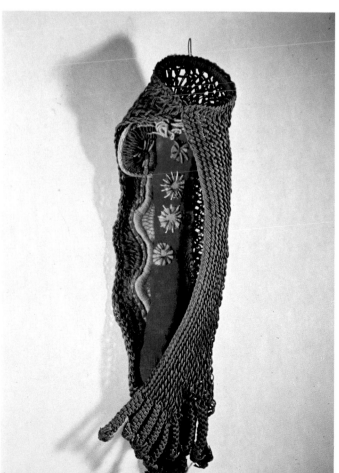

Above: Fish by Lissy Funk. Detail of embroidered tapestry in red, white, blue, and green linen thread embroidered on black linen. Collection Nidau School, Switzerland

Left: Jonah by Alma Lesch. Three-dimensional hanging of plaited yarn, embroidery, and appliqué

Above: Embroidery in Jacobean style designed by the author for a perfume container. Embroidered by Ann Marie Murphy. Reproduced with permission of Avon Products, Inc.

Right: Women by Sylvia Wolff. Wall hanging in appliqué and stitchery.

Opposite, above left: Solomon's Song by Alma Lesch. Irregularly shaped wall hanging of embroidery and appliqué.

Opposite, above right: Detail of a 16' × 4' embroidered tapestry by Lissy Funk. Collection Old Folks' Home, Wollishofen, Zurich, Switzerland

Opposite: The Happy Moment. Embroidered tapestry by Lissy Funk.

Above: Pillow with multicolored embroidery by Helen Bitar.

Opposite: Totem by Memphis Wood. Three-dimensional sculpture of embroidery on fabric stretched and adhered to armatures.

Above: Pillow with multicolored embroidery by Helen Bitar.

Right: Detail of King Florus, an embroidered tapestry by Shirley Marein. Hand-dyed yarn on hand-dyed Duraback ground, with macramé.

Untitled Blues and Browns *by Mariska Karasz. Wall
hanging of stitchery on a hand-dyed, hand-woven background
fabric.* Courtesy Bertha Schaefer Gallery

Above: Fight Smog, Ride a Horse.
Needlepoint and bargello pillow top
by Shirley Marein.

Below: The Sensuous Chair *by Norma*
Minkowitz. Three-dimensional soft
sculpture of appliqué, stitchery, cro-
chet, hooking, and padding.

COMPOSITE STITCHES

INTERLACING: The formation of foundation stitches, in single rows or in series, is the basic structure for interlacing any type of thread or fiber. Unusual fibers, metallic threads, and raffia are suitable for interlacing because it is not necessary to pierce the fabric with these supplementary threads. Many stitches can be used for a foundation: back stitch, running stitch, and herringbone, stem, and star stitches, in addition to others. Experiment with laying parallel bars of thread across the fabric and working some of the complex stitches, such as chain stitch or Cretan stitch, across the bars. Rich textural effects covering large areas are particularly suitable for creating abstract designs in stitchery.

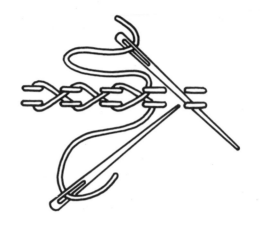

DOUBLE THREADED RUNNING STITCH

INTERLACED BAND STITCH

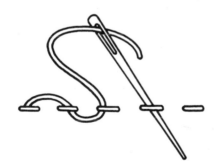

THREADED RUNNING STITCH

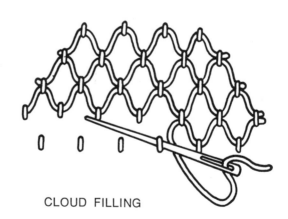

CLOUD FILLING

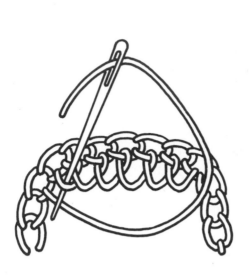

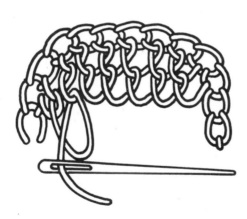

BUTTONHOLE FILLING

Joseph's Coat *by Alma Lesch. Hand-dyed with vegetable and aniline dyes in red-purple, beige, and shades of orange.*

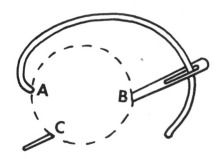

SPIDER'S WEB

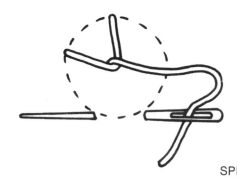
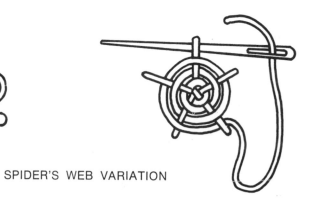

SPIDER'S WEB VARIATION

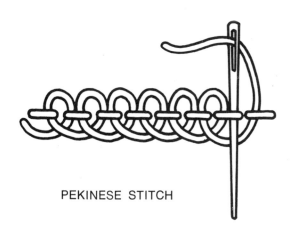

PEKINESE STITCH

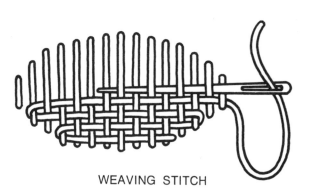

WEAVING STITCH

LAIDWORK AND COUCHING

In laidwork and the couching of fibers, very long stitches laid across a surface for couching or laidwork require fastening to the background fabric. Threads and fibers may be laid in any direction and tied in a variety of ways. Short vertical stitches, horizontal stitches, cross-stitches, and fly stitch are all possible ways to tie down stitches in matching or contrasting colors. Couching and laidwork are very similar, and the terms are sometimes used interchangeably; however "couching" usually implies that a supplementary thread has been used to tie the laid threads down to the background fabric. Couching is notable for its flexibility in fitting a curved line, and its freedom and fluidity in performance are similar to drawing a sweeping line with a crayon. Multiple fibers and cordage may be affixed to a surface invisibly with a fine supplementary couching thread. Medieval church vestments of gold and silver on silk were couched invisibly with linen thread worked from the underside with a separate needle. The supplementary thread comes up and encircles the surface fiber, pulling a small amount of the surface thread down through the same hole from which the supplement emerged. Where each dip occurs on large surface areas, a slight regular or alternating pattern break is visible.

Suburbia *by Florence King Weichsel. Stitchery using appliquéd paisley shawl on linen.* Collection Mr. and Mrs. Donald Blum

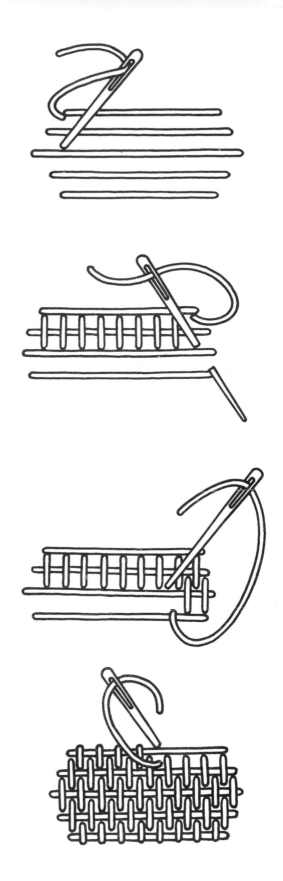

HORIZONTAL LAIDWORK

Lay parallel foundation stitches horizontally or vertically, about ¼″ apart for moderately scaled embroidery and farther apart for large hangings made of heavier cord. Overlay the parallel straight stitches in alternate courses, like bricks. When the overlying stitches are close together, the foundation is barely visible. This stitch, done in one color, may be worked closely as an opaque filling or could be widely spaced for an open effect. With several tints or tones of a single color, gradual shading is possible. Use two needles, introducing each color with a single stitch at the center of a row. Gradually increase the number of stitches in the new color with each new row until there is a full row of the new color.

DIAGONAL LAIDWORK

Lay down a series of diagonal stitches crossing each other. Tie them at the intersections with a small vertical stitch. You might tie the diagonal threads with an upright cross-stitch or use a contrasting color to set off the tying thread.

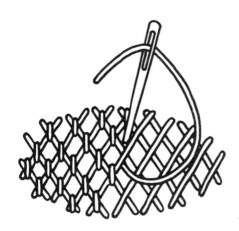

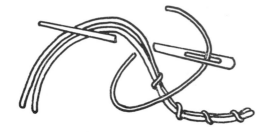

COUCHING

Any number of strands may be couched together. Bring the strands to be couched from the underside of the fabric or simply lay them freely on the surface. If a specific line is to be covered, pin the strands down or use masking tape to hold them in position for couching. Couch with a matching color or a contrasting color. Line up the couching stitches on every row, or alternate each course, as though they were bricks. Return the couching thread to the reverse side and tie it. The strands that are being couched may be returned to the reverse side by threading them back into a needle or by pulling them through with a crochet hook. Should knotting on the reverse side present a problem, apply a small amount of white glue to the knot or the end of the strands with a toothpick.

Vortices *by Cynthia Kendzior.*

RUG STITCHES

TURKEYWORK

This is the basic stitch used in the making of Oriental rugs. It is sometimes called the Ghiordes knot or, in Scandinavia, the Rya knot. Although knotted pile rugs of this type are generally worked on vertical warp threads, the turkeywork stitch may be worked with a needle and thread on embroidery fabric or with a needle and yarn on a rug backing. Uncut turkeywork is often used on embroidery to produce a series of knotted loops to simulate the texture of animal fur. Cut turkeywork when rubbed between the fingers has a soft, fuzzy appearance if it is made with woolen yarn. A strong backing fabric such as monk's cloth or Duraback is suitable for a turkeywork rug. Use two- to six-ply wool, acrylic fiber, or rayon and cotton blends to make rugs. Space each row of stitches ½" apart. It is helpful and convenient to draw a weft thread every sixth row from the rug backing fabric to ensure even, equally spaced rows of turkeywork. Uncut work will produce a series of loops; cut work makes a velvet pile. Loops may be worked to a specific length or to several lengths. To keep lengths even, mark a card to use as a gauge. Cut and trim the loops with rug shears.

Turkeywork rug embroidered with home-spun Mexican wool by Shirley Marein, 1970.

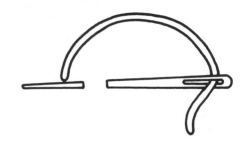

TURKEYWORK (UNCUT)

Knot the end of the thread. Bring the needle up through the fabric. With the thread above the needle, take a straight stitch to the right. Bring the needle point up halfway in the middle of the stitch. Draw the thread through. Hold the thread down with the thumb and bring a loop to the right. Insert the needle at right, making a stitch half the length of the previous one. Draw the needle through, maintaining the depth of the loop with your thumb. Start the second loop with the thread above the needle, as shown in the third drawing.

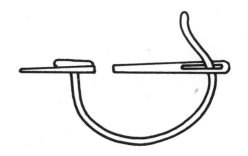

TURKEYWORK (CUT)

Do not place a knot on the end of the thread. Draw the thread through from A to B on the face of the fabric. Hold the end of the thread down with the thumb. With the thread above the needle take a straight stitch to the right. Bring the needle point up halfway between C and B at D. Continue looping as described in turkeywork (uncut). When each row of loops has been completed, cut each loop in the center.

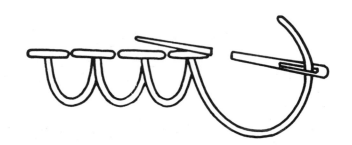

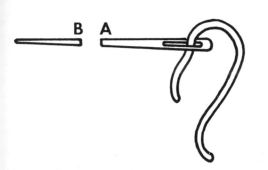

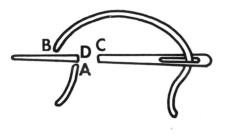

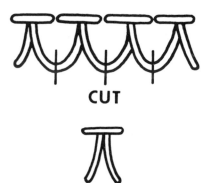

Tree Forms *by Martha Miller, 1970. Rug embroidered in natural-colored Danish wools on linen fabric.*

French needlework in gros point and petit point in the chinoiserie *manner, c. 1740. Collection Irene Stuchell*

EMBROIDERY ON CANVAS

PART II

Needlepoint is embroidery on an open-mesh fabric often referred to as canvas. An open-mesh fabric is one with right-angle intersections that are visible enough to be counted. The intersection is the point at which the weft thread crosses the warp thread. The basic needlepoint stitch is a cross-stitch. Each complete cross-stitch occupying a square area is worked over an intersection. Any geometrically woven background fabric may be used. When the first stitch of the cross-stitch is completed, it is known as the half cross-stitch or tent stitch.

Cross-stitches are rarely seen in medieval embroidery and not at all in earlier embroideries. Although there are some examples of tent stitch on thirteenth- and fourteenth-century English vestments, the stitch did not become popular until the sixteenth century. The most significant single influence on embroidery was probably the creation of the steel needle in England. Refinement of the needle eye further facilitated stitchery by making it possible to work in fine and delicate detail. Petit-point stitches can be worked on gauze of 30 to 40 mesh intersections per inch, which is only a little coarser than the screen in the halftone reproduction in the ordinary newspaper. Representation can be so

Early seventeenth-century embroidery of Columbine done in tent stitch on linen with silk thread. Victoria and Albert Museum

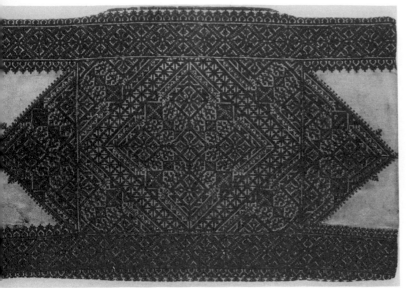

Counted thread needlework on cotton. Berber, nineteenth century.
Collection Mr. and Mrs. William Sadock

Counted thread design on wool fabric from Hungary, about 1920. Collection M. Joan Linden

St. George Slaying the Dragon. *Cross-stitch on fabric, from Macedonia, late nineteenth century.* Collection Vickie Hellmann

minutely detailed as to have the effect of a painting in silk or wool. Many examples of early needlepoint stitchery were worked on loosely woven material, often of coarse linen. On the other hand, the basic stitch can cover a sturdy background canvas totally, producing a most satisfactory upholstery fabric. Double-mesh canvas invented in France, called penelope (in reference to the endless tapestry woven by Penelope as a ruse to put off would-be suitors while she waited for Odysseus's long-delayed return), made the combination of petit point and gros point possible. (Gros point, as opposed to petit point, is commonly called needlepoint today.) Penelope canvas can be spaced by moving the double threads apart with the needle to work the finer detail in petit point, and then using the canvas as it is for the larger, less detailed areas of the background. In some early pieces petit point worked on gauze was inserted or woven into a large-mesh canvas. Embroidery over needlepoint to

Hand-painted needlework design for Berlin woolwork from a German pattern book. Nineteenth century. Collection of the author

depict such fine details as eyes and hair was not uncommon.

Early in the nineteenth century and during the Victorian period needlepoint and cross-stitch patterns were printed and published in Germany. Romantic paintings and brilliant floral designs were copied and adapted to the grids of graph paper. Many of these printed patterns, hand painted in Berlin, were widely distributed in Europe and America. Early examples of Berlin designs were embroidered in silk; however, the breeding of Spanish Merino sheep in Saxony, a division of Germany, shortly produced a very soft, fine wool. Because the wool was sent to Berlin for dyeing, it came to be known as Berlin wool. The finished embroidered designs were called Berlin woolwork. The name of Berlin wool was changed to Zephyr wool with the advent of the First World War. Today Zephyr and Saxony are trade names considered by manufacturers to be synonymous with very fine, soft wool.

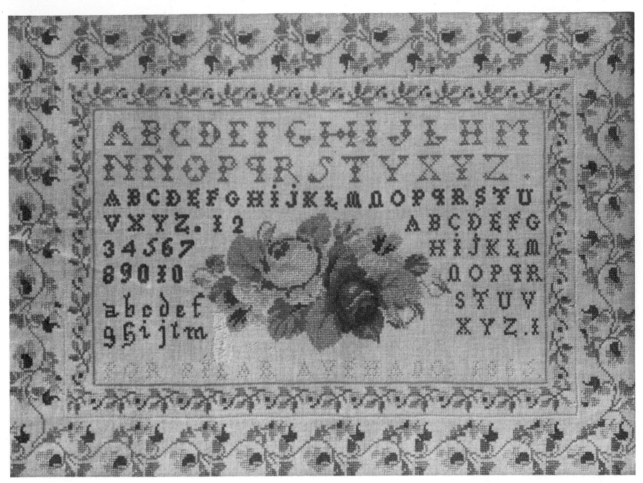

Counted thread sampler with Berlin woolwork floral design, possibly Spanish or Portuguese, dated 1865. Collection of the author

Evening purse worked in petit point, from Germany, about 1914. Collection Hanna Hale

German petit point worked in silk thread on 30-mesh gauze. Late nine-teenth century. Collection Hanna Hale

Contemporary cross-stitch design on fine mesh canvas from the island of Rhodes. Collection of the author

Commemorative needlepoint. Collection of the author

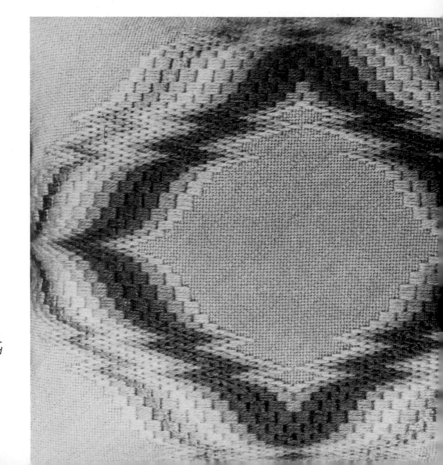

Large unbroken pattern line forming an oval. The interior and background area are filled with needlepoint. Pillow by Lillian Goldman

BARGELLO

Another group of needlepoint stitches popular through the centuries is used in a style known as Hungarian point, bargello, or Florentine embroidery. A great deal of mystery and supposition surrounds the various names; originally these may have designated the pattern source. It is known that Queen Maria Theresa of Hungary was a devotee of the craft, that the Bargello in Florence, formerly an Italian prison and now a national museum, contains some celebrated examples of canvas work, and that Florence was a great cultural center devoted to the textile and decorative arts. Characteristically bargello stitches are parallel to either the warp or weft threads of the canvas and are not worked diagonally as are the traditional tent stitches. Quick and easy to embroider, most of these stitches are worked over four and under two threads of the canvas. Deep space, subtle pattern changes, and delicate shading are suggested by the use of the same or related colors in series of tints or tones repeated at intervals. The design is often established in a single row stitched across the center of the canvas, with all succeeding rows following the pattern of this initial row.

QUICK POINT OR GREAT POINT

These newly coined names apply to needlepoint stitchery on large-mesh canvas. Larger meshes require fewer stitches per inch and are suitable for children's work and rug making. Needlepoint rugs embroidered with heavy rug yarn on large-mesh canvas have been made and used over the centuries, particularly in France.

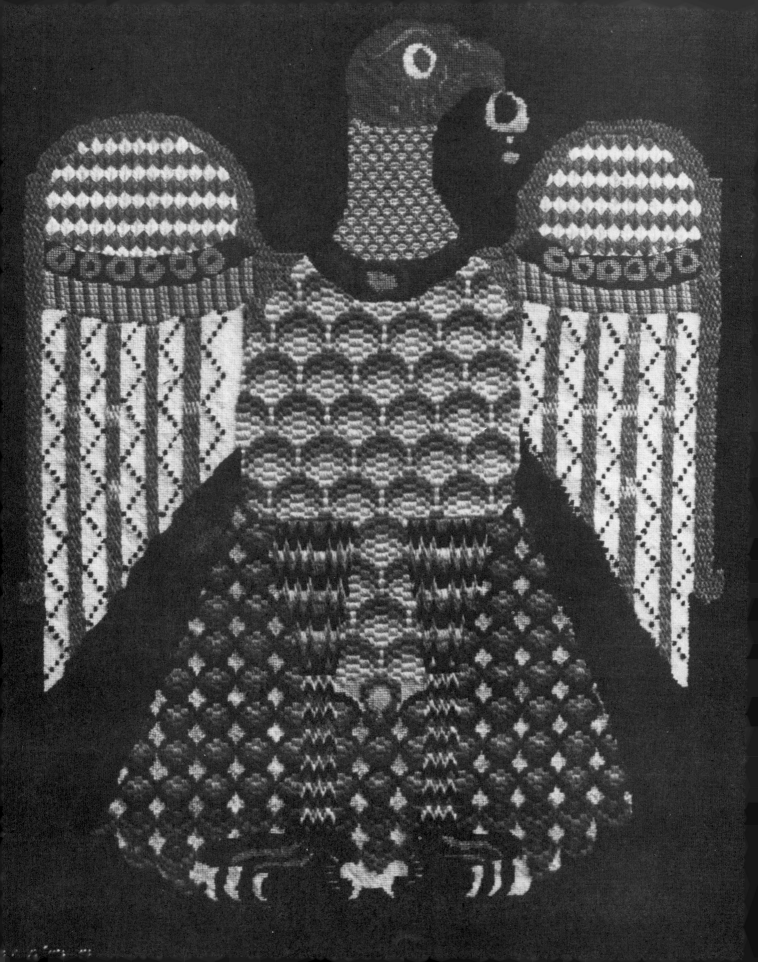

NEEDLE-POINT STITCHES

GLOSSARY

WARP THREADS
Vertical threads running down the canvas.

WEFT THREADS
Horizontal threads running across the canvas.

MESHES
Warp and weft threads surrounding the spaces through which the needle passes form right angles, called mesh intersections. The thread count of canvas can be determined either by the number of intersections or the number of spaces. More intersections per inch require many more and smaller stitches.

PETIT POINT
Very small stitches that may be worked on gauze as fine as 40 mesh per inch. An average petit-point canvas has 20 mesh per inch.

GROS POINT
Larger stitches worked on 8-, 10-, 12-, or 14-mesh canvas and commonly known as needlepoint.

GREAT POINT, QUICK POINT
Very large stitches worked on a 3- to 5-mesh canvas that is used for rugs, in widths up to 60 inches.

BARGELLO
Straight stitches worked parallel to the warp or weft of the canvas. Stitches or groups of stitches are parallel to each other; successive stitches proceed up or down from the previous stitch.

PENELOPE CANVAS
Two-thread or double-thread canvas of cotton or hemp.

MONOCANVAS
Single thread canvas of cotton linen, or hemp in widths from 24" to 54", also called unimesh, monofil, French monocanvas, unicanvas, or congress canvas.

TRAME
A long horizontal running stitch used to indicate the colors and design drawn on a needlepoint canvas, and maintained as an understitching which adds depth and dimension.

Original needlepoint and bargello designs can be easily planned and created on graph paper. Graph paper duplicates the lines and squares of the canvas and can be bought in several grid sizes or adjusted to scale by using two or more squares to equal the size of the canvas mesh. Use colored pencils, watercolors, or felt-tipped markers to indicate designs and color schemes. Cut the graph paper to add insertions or extend the size. Cut out design

Opposite: The Bird by Rosalie Adolf, 1972. Embroidery in petit point, needlepoint, and bargello on 18-mesh monofil canvas, 16" × 20". Inspired by a design woven on a twelfth-century silk chasuble.

Designs for needlepoint and bargello developed on graph paper are flexible and simple to adjust for changes. This lettering is adapted from a type face called Broadway and worked out in colored pencil.

elements and arrange and rearrange them, reassembling sections on another piece of graph paper. Examine all possibilities until you are satisfied with the design.

Select canvas of a mesh size and width suited to the design and purpose of the embroidery. Detailed designs with small areas of descriptive color require more stitches per inch in order to achieve subtle gradations of tone and changes of color. Highly polished threads wear longer. Reject any canvas with flaws or weak threads.

Single thread monocanvas comes in two grades. In one type the warp and weft threads are laid over and under each other. More desirable is monocanvas with a twist in the warp above and below the weft threads. Try to place the design on the straight of the canvas. The design is well placed for stitchery when the selvages are on the right and left and the warping threads run from top to bottom.

Allow 3 inches of extra canvas beyond the design areas for finishing. Fold 1″ masking tape over the cut edges to prevent fraying. Lay the canvas over the drawing and trace the design with a waterproof marker so that it will not bleed through to the woolen surface when moistened during stretching or washing. Should the design be difficult to see through the canvas, prepare a distinct black line diagram on tracing paper for transfer, keeping the original design for color reference. With some experience it is possible to transfer designs by counting the intersections of the graph paper and placing stitches at the corresponding intersections of the canvas. If it is necessary to color areas of the design on the canvas, use thinned acrylic paints.

Use a No. 18 blunt tapestry needle for 12-mesh canvas. Smaller blunt needles are suitable for finer meshes. Two-ply tapestry yarn gives good coverage, as does Persian wool, a

Freely interpreted rendering of the graph paper design in needlepoint and bargello. Designed by the author

two-ply three-strand yarn easily separated into single strands. Silk and cotton flosses provide interesting texture changes. D.M.C. cotton floss is lustrous and comes in many colors with an extensive range of tints and tones. Yarn and thread should be cut in lengths of 18" to 24". Longer lengths are less economical because of the abrasion caused by the coarse canvas. If two strands of Persian yarn are recommended, use a one-yard strand through the needle eye, doubled over on itself. There are no discernible right and wrong sides to the canvas. Knotted ends are undesirable. A neat, flat reverse side will ensure smooth perfection on the front surface. Run the yarn through several meshes of the canvas. Succeeding stitches will cover the starting yarn and hold it firm. Once the work is begun, new yarn can be run through several stitches on the reverse side and ended in the same manner. Clip any extremely long ends. Perfect a smooth, rhythmical working technique. Maintain uniformity in the direction of all slanted and crossed stitches for a final even appearance.

Great care should be taken to minimize the possibility of distortion. Work different areas of canvas rather than proceeding from one edge or corner to the other. Although a single thrust of the needle from top surface to top surface may save time, stabbing the needle up and down in two strokes helps to relieve the pull on the warp and weft of the canvas.

Blocking is usually necessary to return the canvas to its original shape. It is a good idea to record the desired size and form by drawing it on a piece of paper. Place the paper with the drawn size on a piece of pressed board or a drawing board and check the distortion of the finished canvas against the drawing. Place the canvas face up or face down on a clean surface and lightly sprinkle it with cool water. Tack the edges down, alternating from side to side, pulling the canvas into shape until it conforms to the outline. Do not use staples or

Fitting the finished canvas to the size record drawn on white paper.

The finished canvas tacked down for blocking.

tacks that have a tendency to rust. Allow the canvas to dry thoroughly. It is also possible to block needlework on an artists' canvas stretcher. Should cleaning be necessary, dip the canvas into a basin of cold water to which a small amount of a very mild detergent such as Woolite has been added. Just swing the canvas from side to side; do not wring or twist it. Rinse it in cold water, pat it dry with a bath towel, then stretch it. Washing may take some of the sizing out of the canvas; this can be reapplied on the back during blocking. Light surface sponging or cleaning by an expert is less damaging. Lost stiffness is not important in a framed picture, but washed rugs and handbags may become unattractively limp and distorted. Muslin tacked over the finished parts of the needlepoint will keep it clean as you work.

Needlepoint intended for upholstery is best applied by professional upholsterers, but footstools and removable chair seats can be done at home. The finished canvas should be a little bit larger all around to allow for complete coverage of the upholstered surface. Arrange the canvas over the surface and hold it in position with straight pins at the center and corners. Turn the pad or seat bottom side up and tack the canvas from side to side, pulling it tight. Do not push tacks in fully until the needlepoint is arranged evenly and satisfactorily.

Pillow top sampler by Eileen Goldman

Select a fabric backing for pillow covers. Self-welting or cording is easy to make by cutting bias strips from the backing material, wrapping it over soft cord, and sewing close to the cord on the sewing machine, using the single welting foot. Sew this cording, finished side in, to the edge of the finished canvas. Place the backing fabric and finished canvas with right sides together and the cording inside and baste, leaving one side open for turning. Machine sew the three basted sides together. Sew the cording to one side of the open end. Turn the cover right side out. Insert the pillow and hand slip-stitch the opening together close to the cording, or add a zipper, following instructions on the packet. Professional results can be achieved, particularly with circular pillows, by sewing a muslin pillow casing and filling it with polyester fiber after it is inserted in the cover. Fill firmly, then slip-stitch first the casing and finally the embroidered covering.

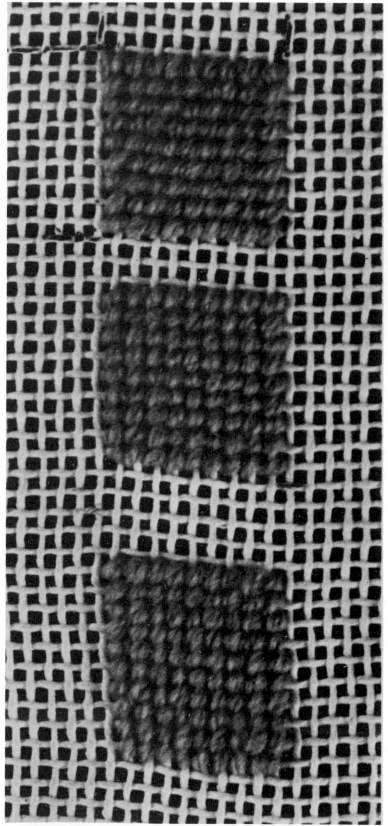

Needlepoint examples worked by Jan Silberstein

APPROXIMATE YARN GAUGE FOR BACKGROUND STITCHES

CONTINENTAL STITCH
3 strands of Persian yarn on 10-mesh canvas, 42″ of yarn per square inch.

BASKETWEAVE STITCH
3 strands of Persian yarn on 10-mesh canvas, 32″ of yarn per square inch.

HALF CROSS-STITCH
3 strands of Persian yarn on 10-mesh canvas, 24″ of yarn per square inch.

To determine yarn quantities for large backgrounds, measure the width and length of the canvas area in inches. Multiply the width by the length. Make an approximate measurement of the subject matter and subtract this figure from the total measurement of the canvas. Multiply the final total by the number of inches of yarn required to fill a one-inch sample swatch. Divide the total by 36 to convert inches into yardage. It is advisable to work test squares for different stitches, yarns, and canvas sizes.

CANVAS STITCHES

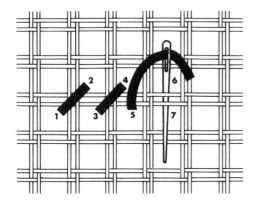

HALF CROSS-STITCH

Simplest of all needlepoint stitches is the half cross-stitch. Less wool is used because the back is not fully covered. The finished needlepoint therefore does not make sturdy upholstery covering. Always work from left to right, starting at the bottom of the stitch. Cross diagonally over one mesh intersection of the canvas, inserting the needle in the row above. Bring the needle point up again in the opening directly below. Always insert the needle vertically. At the end of a completed row turn the work upside down so that the next row can also be worked from left to right. Three strands of Persian wool covers well on 10-mesh canvas, as does six-ply rug wool on 5-mesh canvas. It is advisable to work the half cross-stitch on penelope canvas. The double-thread warp and weft help to minimize the distortion to be expected when rows are worked continuously in one direction.

CONTINENTAL STITCH

Similar in appearance to the half cross-stitch, the continental stitch fully covers the back of the work. It requires about twice as much wool. Because of the greater durability provided by the fully covered back, this stitch is suitable for chair seats, rugs, and upholstery. Work rows from right to left. Bring the needle up at 1; crossing the intersection diagonally, insert the needle at 2. Bring the needle up at 3, to the left of 1. Work in horizontal rows, turning the canvas upside down for each new row. The continental stitch is suitable for filling large areas and backgrounds as well as outlining forms, and it works well with three strands of Persian wool on 10-mesh canvas. The canvas has a tendency to pull out of shape, but it can be stretched back into shape by blocking when the embroidery is done.

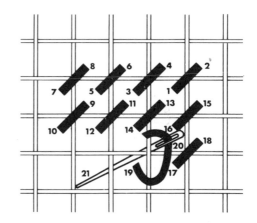

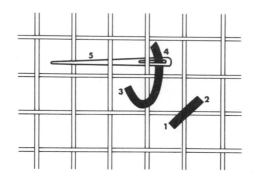

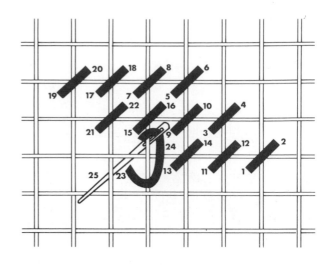

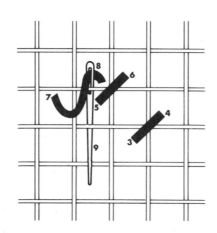

BASKETWEAVE STITCH

In appearance, basketweave stitch is the same as the continental or half cross-stitch; however, it is worked in diagonal rows rather than horizontally or vertically, resulting in a firm construction and an even regularity. This stronger construction lessens the tendency of the canvas to stretch out of shape. The work does not have to be turned upside down for each row. Begin the first row at the lower right-hand corner of the canvas and proceed diagonally upward, bringing the needle in and out horizontally for each new stitch on the way upward, and in and out vertically on the following row as it proceeds downward. Basketweave is excellent for filling large areas, although it is not quite flexible enough for working out intricate design areas. The half cross-stitch and the continental stitch can be used to work around intricate areas, with the basketweave stitch used to fill large backgrounds.

Fuller coverage can be achieved by starting the diagonal ascent of this stitch on a mesh intersection in which the vertical warp thread rises over the horizontal weft thread.

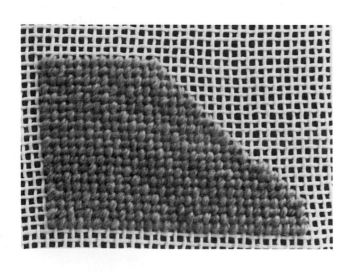

Landscape *by Pauline Shapiro. Cross-stitch on fine cotton mesh canvas, embroidered with cotton floss.*

CROSS-STITCH

Always a favorite, cross-stitch adds texture to a design. It can be slanted over one horizontal and one vertical mesh or doubled in size, crossing two horizontal and two vertical meshes. The cross-stitches on small design areas should be completed individually. Large background areas are best worked in a row of half cross-stitches, completing the second half of the stitch on the return row. All stitches must cross in the same direction for an even appearance. A raised dimensional effect can be achieved with tramé understitching. Vary the lengths of the tramé understitching, starting and stopping successive rows in different places to avoid the formation of unwanted patterns behind the cross-stitches. Elaborate on cross-stitches by experimenting with tall and narrow stitches, upright crosses, the Smyrna cross-stitch (which combines the diagonal and upright cross-stitch), and many other combinations.

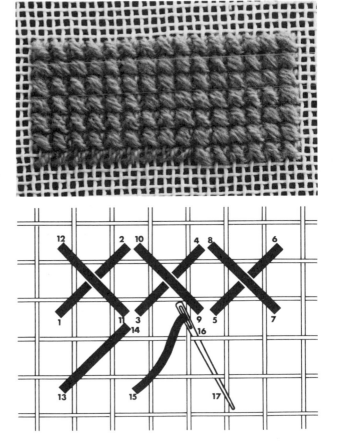

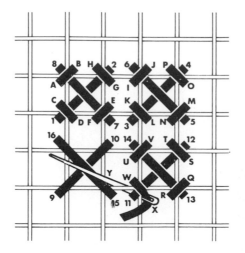

RICE STITCH (WILLIAM AND MARY or CROSSED CORNERS STITCH)

Basically a cross-stitch, worked over two horizontal and two vertical meshes, rice stitch has a diagonal top stitch added to each corner. The small corner stitch is effective worked in a contrasting color. Use three-strand Persian wool on 10-mesh canvas for the cross and a single strand for the corner stitch.

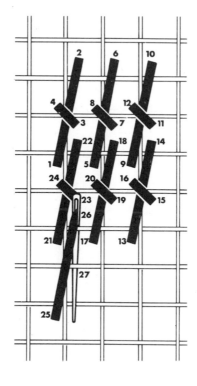

KNOTTED STITCH

A long slanted stitch worked over three weft threads and across a single warp thread, with a short top stitch crossing the center in the opposite direction. Visually the effect is of a center knot, but the stitch is tied down rather than knotted. Work each stitch individually before proceeding to the next. Work in horizontal rows without turning the canvas. The rows can be of contrasting colors. Use three strands of Persian yarn on 10-mesh canvas.

DOUBLE LEVIATHAN STITCH

Begin with a large cross-stitch worked over four horizontal and vertical meshes. Four more diagonal cross-stitches are added as shown, ending with an upright cross-stitch on the top. The double leviathan stitch is raised and decorative. A long straight stitch or back stitch may be added between rows for more adequate canvas coverage. These stitches, as well as the upright cross-stitch topping the double leviathan stitch, may be worked in contrasting colors.

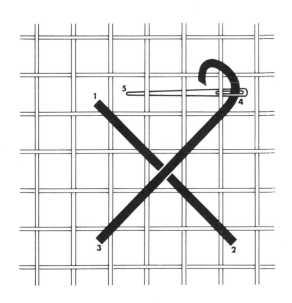

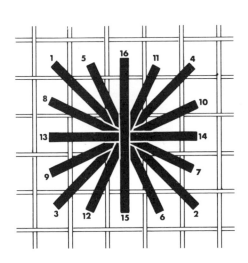

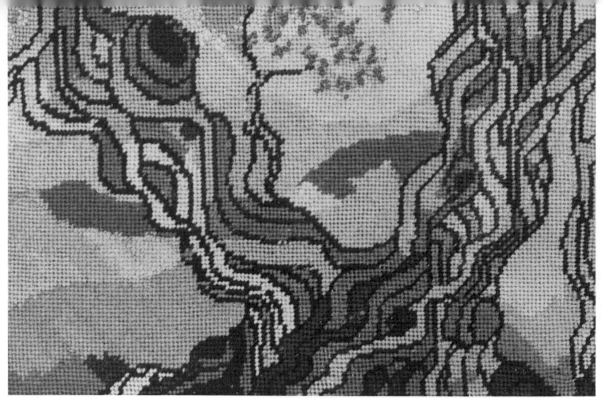

To Thenthron, Olive Tree, Crete *by Harriet Pomerance. Basketweave and continental stitch on monofil canvas, embroidered with French knots.*

WEB STITCH

The web stitch is tied down at each intersection of the canvas in a technique similar to that of couching in embroidery. The stitch has a woven appearance. When worked in two colors, it looks like tweed. It is not suitable for backgrounds, but adds texture to small areas. Lay long stitches on the diagonal, completing the short top stitches across each one before proceeding to the next. Two strands of Persian wool are suitable for 10-mesh canvas.

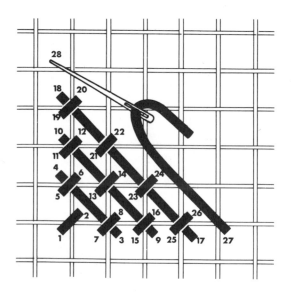

STRAIGHT GOBELIN STITCH
(UPRIGHT GOBELIN or RENAISSANCE
STITCH)

Called Gobelin for the tapestry establishment in France, this is a very old stitch with many variations. It closely resembles the tapestry weave. Use three strands of Persian wool for full coverage. Tramé can be used to emphasize dimension by making a raised ridge. Work over two weft threads, bringing the needle up from between two warp threads at the top or bottom of the row. Start each new stitch at either the top or bottom, but keep the same needle movements throughout for an even appearance, turning the canvas for each row. As you work, stop occasionally and allow the needle to hang down so that the thread untwists.

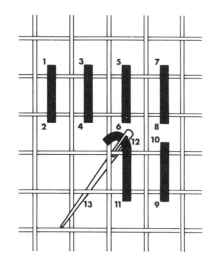

SLANTED GOBELIN STITCH (OBLIQUE GOBELIN)

Slanted Gobelin covers the canvas more adequately than upright Gobelin. Work in horizontal rows, starting the first row from left to right. The stitch is worked from top to bottom of the area to be covered. Bring the needle up at 1, at the right of a warp thread, then take a diagonal stitch down across two weft threads to 2 and insert the needle on the left side of the same warp thread. For the next stitch, bring the needle up at 3, which is two weft threads up and two warp threads to the right of 2. The second row is worked from right to left, inserting the needle downward from above rather than upward from below. The stitch resembles tent stitch. It may be worked over two warp threads and as many as five weft threads.

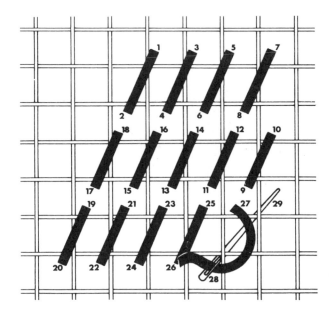

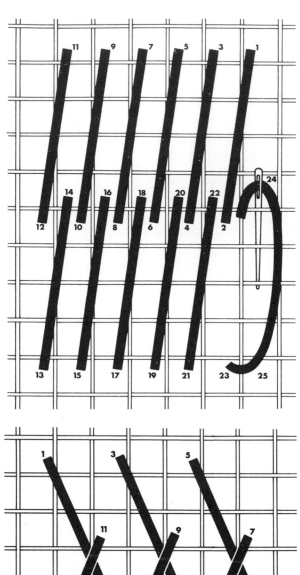

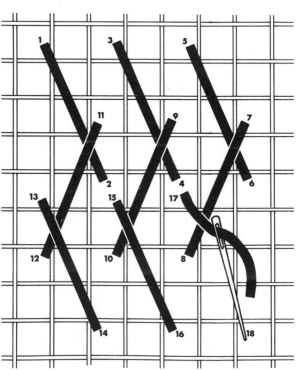

ENCROACHING GOBELIN STITCH (INTERLOCKED GOBELIN STITCH)

Dovetailing the stitches produces a woven effect rather than the usual ribbed appearance. Because the stitch is slanted, it is possible to overlap the second row. This longer slanted stitch passes across only one warp thread but may cover from two to five weft threads. Each row fits between the stitches of the previous row. Rows are worked alternately from left to right and right to left. Use two colors, if desired, by working the first row from left to right, starting at the bottom of each stitch. Select a second color and start again at the bottom left of the next row, working toward the right. This is an excellent background stitch; it works up rapidly.

PLAITED GOBELIN STITCH

Full, soft, and cushiony, the plaited Gobelin stitch looks woven and is very decorative on large surfaces. It takes five or six strands of Persian wool to get full coverage on a 10-mesh canvas. Experiment with other types of wool for this stitch. Work over four horizontal weft threads and two vertical warp threads of the canvas, then go back and forth across the rows, covering each slanted stitch of the previous row. Overlap the top part of each stitch across two weft threads, alternating the slant of each row.

HORIZONTAL MOSAIC STITCH

Mosaic stitches come in many variations that combine long and short slanted stitches. The horizontal mosaic stitch is worked across the canvas in horizontal rows, with one short stitch over one mesh, one long stitch over two meshes, and then one more short stitch to complete a square. Using two colors for alternate squares creates a checkerboard pattern. For this effect use two needles, one for each color.

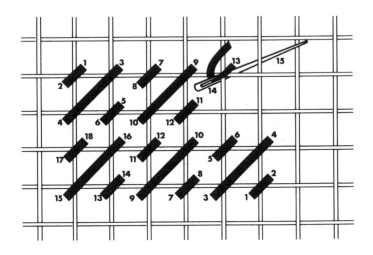

DIAGONAL MOSAIC STITCH

Start at the bottom right and work diagonally across and upward to the left side; then turn the canvas upside down for the second row and start again at the bottom right-hand side, working upward toward the left. A diagonal pattern will form. The use of two colors accentuates the diagonal appearance. If a second color is used, thread two needles, each with a different color, starting each color at the bottom and working upward. Mosaic stitches form a firm backing, assuring better wear.

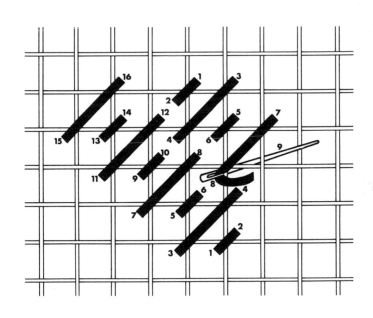

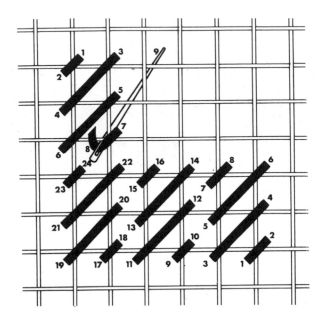

CASHMERE STITCH

The cashmere stitch is another in the long-and-short family. Composed of one short, two long, and one short stitch worked over two mesh intersections, it forms an oblong. Work the first short stitch from left to right on the first mesh of the right-hand corner, turning the canvas for each new row. This stitch worked in units fills rectangular or square areas effectively.

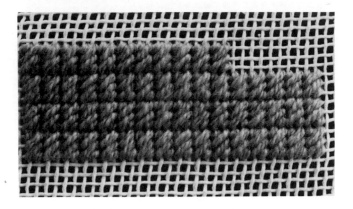

SCOTCH STITCH (CHECKER STITCH)

The Scotch stitch is similar to the mosaic stitch. The first stitch is over one mesh intersection, the second over two intersections, the third over three intersections, then the fourth over two and the fifth over one mesh intersection, completing a square. It is sometimes called the *checker stitch* because the squares, when done in two colors, form an obvious checkerboard. Subtle variations can be made by alternating the types of stitches in each square. Alternate the Scotch stitch with tent stitch or straight Gobelin stitch.

Butterfly in three-dimensional silhouetted needlepoint by Ronnie Schiller.

BYZANTINE STITCH

Once started, the Byzantine stitch is easy to follow and easy to remember. Diagonal stitches form a pronounced zigzag pattern. Start the zigzag at the top left side, working over two mesh intersections; complete four slanted stitches horizontally and four slanted stitches vertically, four across, four down, four across, four down. The second and subsequent rows can be filled in to fit the first, proceeding either up or down the zigzag. The stitch can be worked over three or four mesh intersections. Five or six stitches in each direction are more suitable for the longer lengths. If the stitch is used as a background filling, graduated stitches may be necessary to fill the corners. Contrasting colors or groups of four or five rows in tonal shading are interesting. Use three strands of Persian wool on 10-mesh canvas.

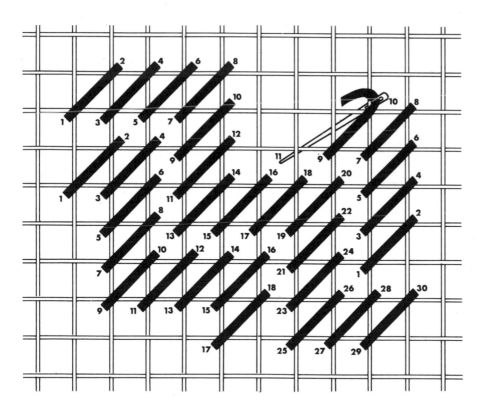

TRIANGLE STITCH

A perfect little 10-mesh square is formed by symmetrically working a graduated series of straight stitches over two to five weft threads from the outside toward the center. Fill out the corners with small cross-stitches in a matching or contrasting color. Square areas easily form a checkerboard. Consider outlining the natural divisions between each unit with a straight stitch. Turn the canvas to work each quarter more easily. Large-mesh canvas may require up to six strands of Persian wool to be covered adequately.

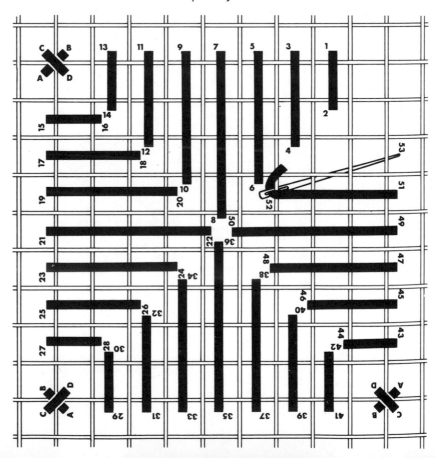

LEAF STITCH

Easily recognizable by its descriptive name, this intriguing stitch, used on a large scale or in multiples of individual units, is a simple way to suggest trees, shrubs, feathers, and similar representational forms. Enlarge or reduce its over-all size as desired. If it is to be used on a functional piece, the problem of snagging should be taken into consideration.

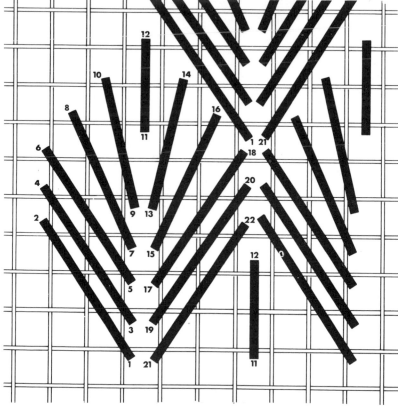

BRIGHTON STITCH

Possibly of English origin, this early nineteenth-century stitch forms an interesting and very pleasant pattern when worked in one or two colors. Although the finished stitch appears to occupy a square area, it is best to work it as a diamond, as shown on the diagram. Work the top half across the row first from left to right, then return, completing the lower half from right to left. The center is filled with an upright cross-stitch.

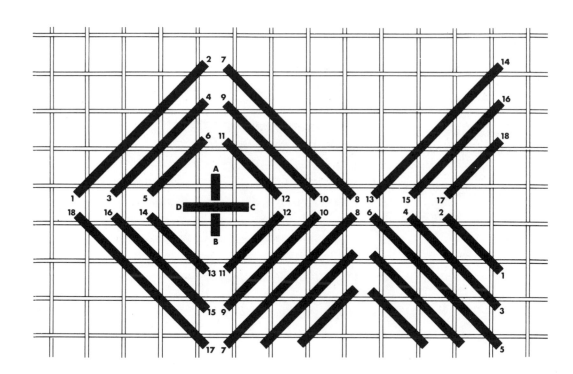

CLOSED FLY WITH STRAIGHT STITCH TRIANGLES

Fly stitch is a traditional embroidery stitch adapted to canvas and combined here with straight stitches graduated to form triangles. Useful for filling large surfaces needing texture or color variety, the fly stitch is a straight stitch worked over two warp threads and tied down over the center with a straight stitch crossing the weft of the row below. Work the straight stitch triangles alongside the fly stitches, coming up with the needle on the odd numbers and going down on the even numbers.

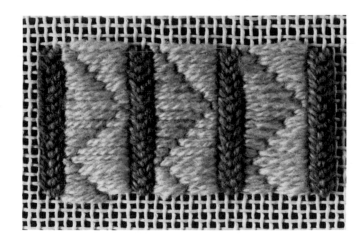

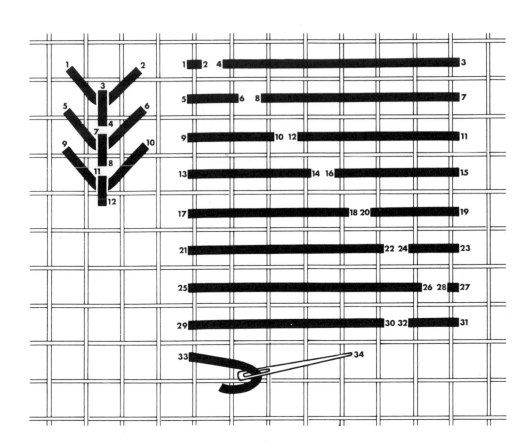

CABLE STITCH

The photographed example of cable stitch is striped in a combination of six-strand cotton floss and two strands of Persian wool for sharp definition and contrasting texture. The stripes can be varied in width, color, and fiber. The stitches are horizontal and all the same length, alternating each row over two warp threads. Because two threads are worked through each space, great care must be taken not to split the threads. The short stitches shown at the ends of rows on the diagram are necessary to fill out an alternating pattern. Turn the canvas upside down to start the second double row.

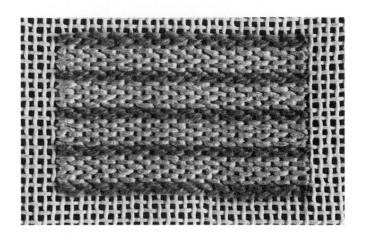

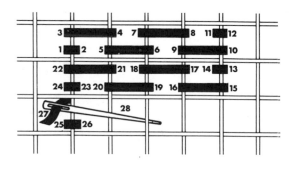

Baseball Player. *Needlepoint embroidery on penelope canvas worked by a young man, aged ten.*

CUSHION STITCH

Form neat little cushions by alternating slanted straight stitches of graduated size. The stitches are raised by working over a ground of tramé, indicated on the diagram by a long straight diagonal stitch labeled Y to X. If two colors are used as shown, the tramé ground is more effective laid under only one of the colors. Match the color of tramé ground to the top stitch. Each cushion stitch slanting to the right can be worked in horizontal rows. Cushion stitches slanting to the left are worked from the bottom of the unit to the top. With one color, the tramé ground can be laid in the form of a cross over units of four cushion stitches and worked from the top or the bottom, but work then proceeds very slowly. Very long rows of tramé grounding are difficult to control.

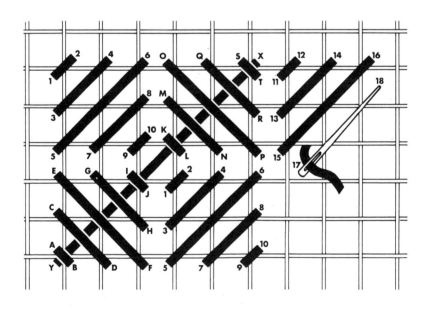

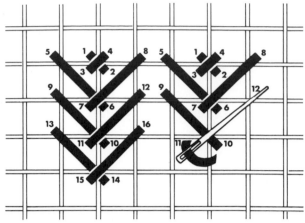

FERN STITCH

Somewhat thinner than its embroidery counterpart fishbone stitch, fern stitch produces strongly ridged vertical stripes. Start with a small cross-stitch. Always work from top to bottom. Use a single color, alternate colors, or select a medley of colors.

HUNGARIAN POINT

This series of alternating short and long stitches forms small diamonds. Work the first stitch over two weft threads, the second over four, and the third over two weft threads, then skip a mesh opening and start the series of three stitches again. Turn the canvas upside down on the second row. Starting on the right again, fill out the alternating row with a short stitch over the first two weft threads, marked on the diagram as X and Y. Skip a mesh opening and start the series of stitches. Work back and forth across the canvas, filling out the indentations at the edges with short stitches. Work all in one color or alternate colors with each row.

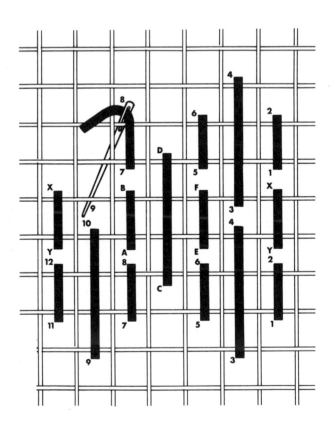

HUNGARIAN GROUNDING

This stitch combines the zigzag pattern of bargello and the diamond shape of Hungarian point. Start at the bottom right-hand corner with a row of vertical stitches, each worked over four weft threads. Move down one mesh opening at a time for three stitches, then continue two stitches upward, two down, and two up again all across the design area. Turn the canvas upside down and work the second row with a row of Hungarian point, with each grouping separated by a space. The next bargello row will fill the opening. Many pattern arrangements in two or three colors are possible. Consider several shades of one color for less contrast between rows or use various colors close in value when working large surfaces.

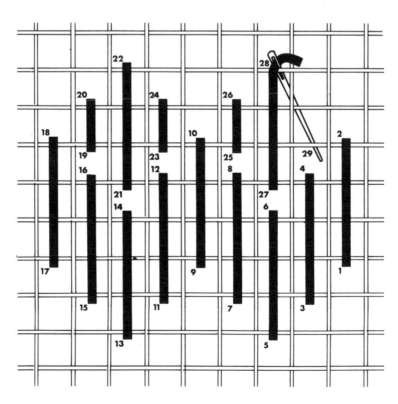

MILANESE STITCH

A stitch with a strong diagonal thrust is worked here in contrasting colors. The direction of the points of the four-stitch triangles reverses with each row. The stitch can be started in either the lower right- or upper left-hand corner. In either case, small stitches are needed to fill out the edge. When the stitch is worked in one color, proceed from right to left in diagonal rows. Take a stitch backward over one intersection, advance and work back over four intersections, alternating one and four intersections on the first row. Alternate two and three intersections on the second row, three and two on the third row, and four and one on the fourth row. Turn the work around on alternate rows in order to work back and forth. The stitch has a tendency to snag when used on pieces receiving considerable wear. Care must be taken to avoid pulling the canvas background out of shape. Work the needle up and down rather than diagonally as you proceed from stitch to stitch.

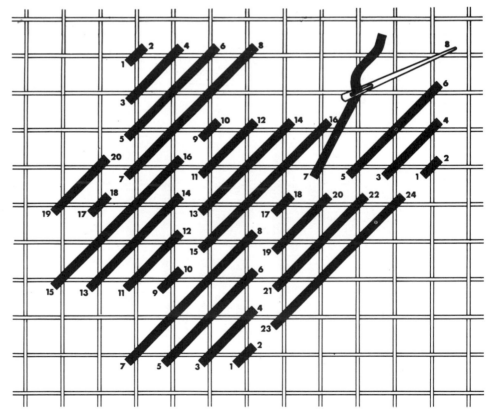

PERSPECTIVE STITCH

Create an illusion of small blocks by using two contrasting colors, one for the top of the box, the other for the base. Work two groups of opposing diagonal stitches, each stitch over two intersections. The number of stitches down must approximate those of the width to keep the shape of the box. Alternate rows must be started three mesh openings from the edge to maintain the illusion. Fill the edges with a tent or straight Gobelin stitch, in a third color if desired.

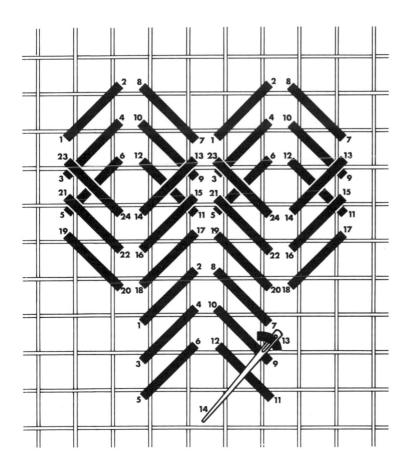

Portrait by Mrs. Robert McGregor.

RAY STITCH

Radiate a fan in any direction from a single starting point. The pattern is more clearly defined when done with two strands of Persian wool on 10-mesh canvas, working through four mesh openings across and down. Greater width and depth mean that more threads must radiate from a single opening and a larger canvas mesh is required to accommodate them. As with all stitches that do not come up and go down over every intersection, complete coverage of the canvas can be accomplished only by not stretching the yarn to its fullest. Allow the yarn to be relaxed but at the same time firm. Work from the outer arms of the fan toward the center.

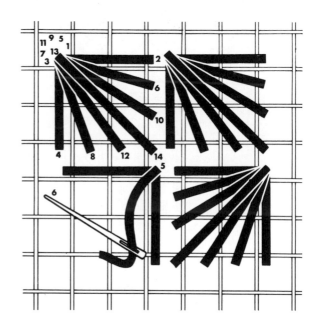

SHADOW MESH

This three-color pattern of alternating diamonds and zigzag straight stitches is also interesting in three values of a single tone. Work the center diamond vertically, remembering to divide the long central stitch in half to make a gentle transition from one color to another.

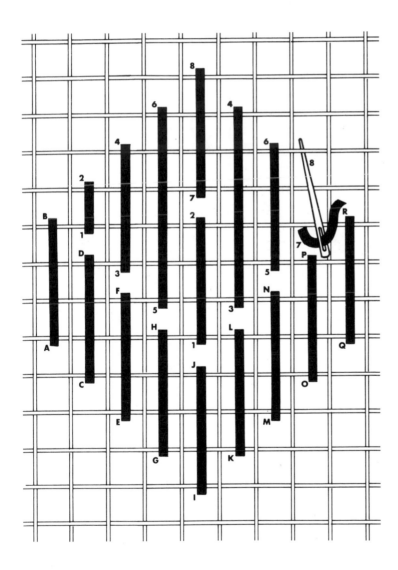

SOUTHERN CROSS

A strikingly handsome raised diamond atop a square base creates an illusion of great depth. The appearance is deceptively complex for a stitch remarkably easy to work. Remember to bring the needle up on the odd numbers and down on the even numbers. Do not pull too tightly. The thread will not fully cover the reverse side, but the raised edge prevents undue abrasion.

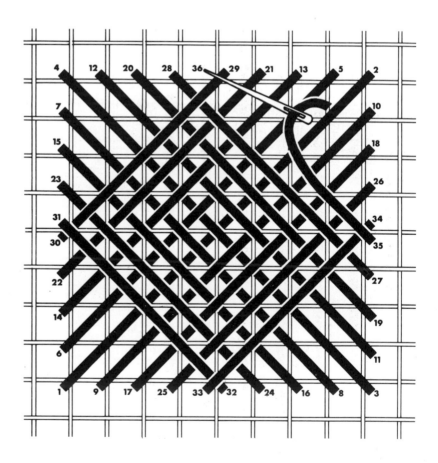

DUTCH STITCH

Names of stitches are puzzling. At times descriptive, they are more often an indication of source. Here we have a very old stitch that may have been recorded in the notebook of an embroiderer from the Netherlands. It is a series of broad cross-stitches with straight stitches in contrasting color overlaying the meeting point of the cross. The large scale and bold color contrast make this a thoroughly contemporary stitch.

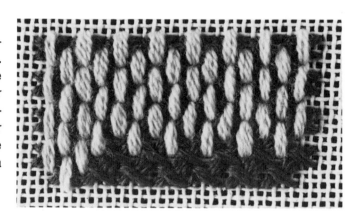

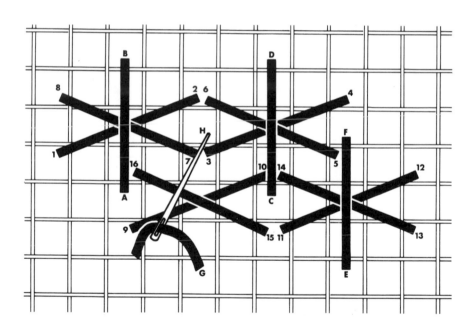

VELVET STITCH

With this stitch you can imitate the woven pile of an Oriental rug, using a loop of any depth topped with a cross-stitch for security. Use penelope canvas for extra strength and nonslippage of warp threads. Work a half cross-stitch over a single intersection, then repeat the movement, making another half cross-stitch into the same meshes, but don't pull it all the way through; leave a loose loop. Complete the cross-stitch, locking the loop in place. Make the loops any desired length. Continue to the end of the row, finishing with two cross-stitches on the opposite selvage. Loops may be left uncut or sheared with a rug scissors to make a velvet pile. Use six-ply rug yarn.

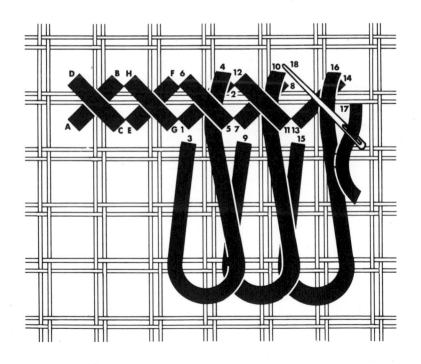

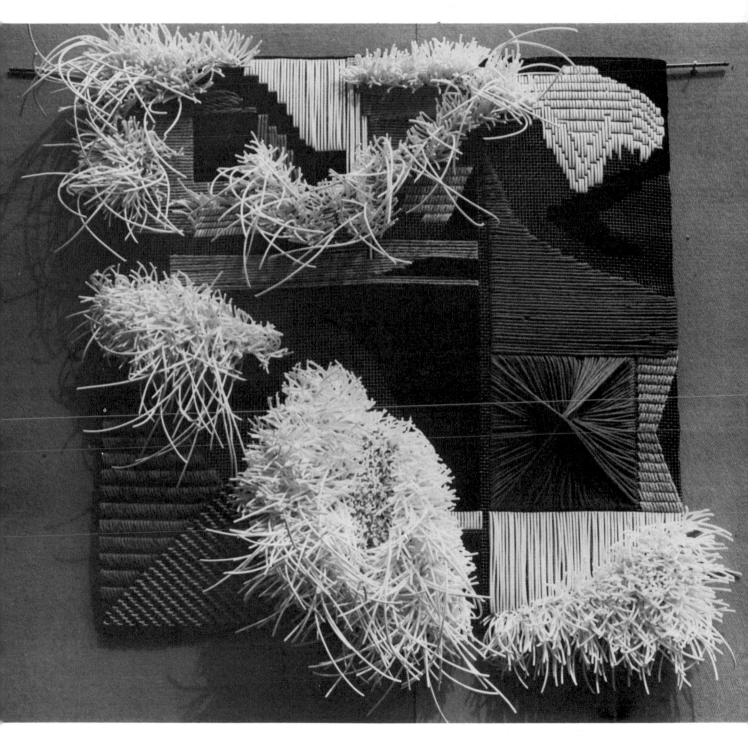

Bangtails *by Jan Silberstein. Needlepoint worked with jute, wool, and polyester welting cord on chicken wire.*

LEFT-HANDED NEEDLEPOINT

Craft and needlework instructions are usually detailed for the right-handed person. Most left-handers have adjusted to the right-handed world. With some previous experience in stitchery, the left-hander will read the instructions, study the diagrams, and proceed automatically, but the finished piece often is a mirror image of the work of right-handers. Noticeable only in a large background of tent stitches, the difference does not affect the quality of the work. Diagrams and illustrative photographs usually show the half cross-stitch, continental stitch, and basketweave stitch slanting from left to right.

For the left-handed needlepointer wishing to work from diagrams and instructions proceeding from left to right, here is the way to work the three basic background stitches:

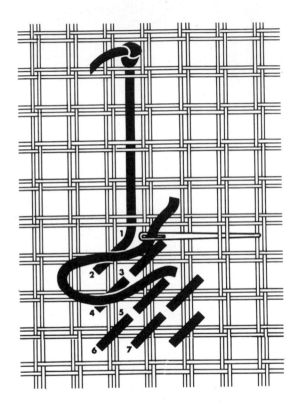

HALF CROSS-STITCH

VERTICAL ROWS: Knot the end of the yarn and start on the left-hand side with a running stitch coming from any direction. This running stitch will be covered later by other stitches; remember to cut off the knot before the stitches are worked over the entire running stitch. If the knot is on the back, it may be removed later or left in the work.

ROW 1. Work from the top down. Bring the needle to the front of the canvas in the first space of the area to be worked. Insert the needle point to the left of the first mesh intersection in the row below, bringing the point up to the right of the intersection. The needle will be in a horizontal position. Draw it through.

ROW 2. Turn the work upside down and repeat the first row. Stop before the last stitch is completed and turn the canvas upside down again.

ROW 3. Complete the last stitch of the previous row by inserting the needle point in the last space to the left of the mesh intersection, bringing the point up to the right of the intersection. Continue down the row.

HORIZONTAL ROWS:
ROW 1. Working from the bottom up, bring the needle point up in the first space of the area to be worked. Cross the intersection to the row above. Holding the needle vertically, point down, insert it under the weft threads. Draw it through to complete the stitch. Do not complete last stitch in Row 1.

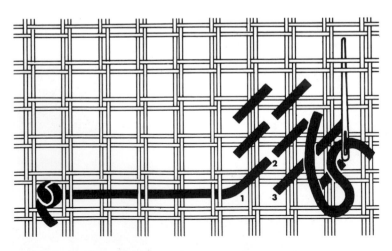

ROW 2. Before the last stitch is completed, turn the work upside down. Cross the intersection with the thread to complete the stitch from the row above; holding the needle vertically, insert it under the weft threads of the row below. Draw through and continue across, repeating Row 1.

CONTINENTAL STITCH

ROW 1. Start on the left-hand side with a knotted running stitch, coming up on the right side of the starting intersection. Bring the thread back and down one row, to the left of the intersection. Come up again two mesh openings to the right in the row above. Continue to the end of the row. Complete the last stitch by inserting the needle vertically under the weft threads, emerging in the mesh opening above. On all turning stitches at the end of rows, stab the needle down and then up.

ROW 2. Turn the canvas upside down on the second row. Remember the left-hander working the continental stitch with a slant to the right must start the stitch each time from the top and complete it below and to the left. Complete the last stitch, before the turn, by bringing the needle point out, under the weft threads, to the mesh opening directly below.

ROW 3. Turn the work upside down and repeat Row 1.

It is advisable for left-handers to work the half cross-stitch and continental stitch on penelope canvas, because crossing an intersection where the weft is laid over the warp on a single-thread canvas with an untwisted warp allows the thread to slip down into the next stitch.

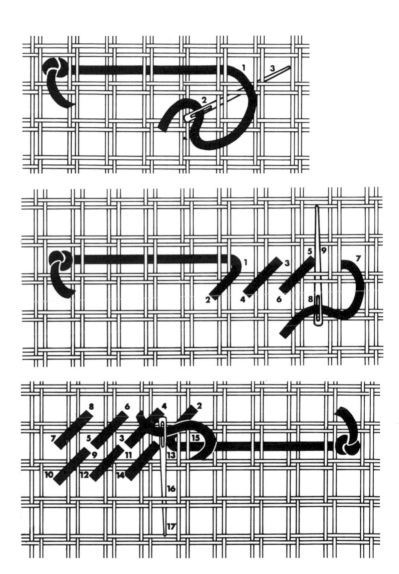

BASKETWEAVE STITCH

ROW 1. Start on the left-hand side with a knotted running stitch, coming up on the right side of the mesh intersection, a row above the running stitch. Take the yarn back over the intersection to the left and insert the needle in the row below. Point the needle upward in a vertical position, bringing the point up from under the two weft threads above. Draw it through. As the diagonal stitches proceed upward, the needle is always parallel to the warp or vertical threads of the canvas. At the top of the row proceed diagonally under the canvas to the right to start the next row.

ROW 2. Take the yarn diagonally down over one mesh intersection to the left. Insert the needle in the row below with the point emerging horizontally from under two warp threads of the canvas.

ROW 3. Repeat the first row.

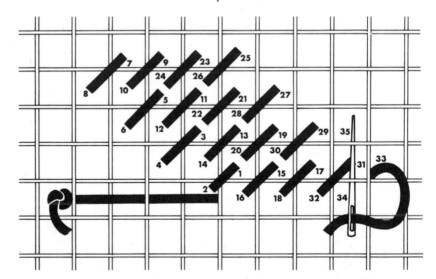

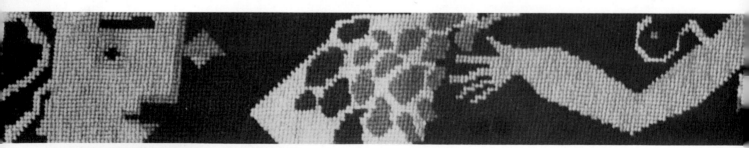

Untitled needlepoint panel by Shirley Marein.

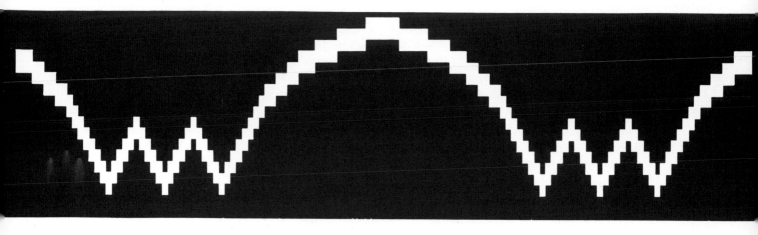

BARGELLO

The fascination of bargello, at times known as Florentine or Hungarian point embroidery, is age-old and compelling. Its continuous popularity is due to the speed with which the stitch can be worked and to the ease with which an infinite variety of designs may be created. The stitch is upright and worked in diagonal groupings across the surface. The counted thread stitches may be worked over any number of weft threads. Most usually they are taken over four weft threads and under two, advancing up or down—the stitches are generally four mesh openings long, and each step begins two mesh openings above or below the previous one. The stitch may also be worked in a combination of long and short stitches or in stitches of graduated length. The design is often established in the first row, with succeeding rows following this set pattern. The very popular flickering patterns that appear to rise and fall rhythmically are known as *flame stitches,* but the name describes the pattern rather than the individual stitch.

Bargello stitchery produces a very firm, durable surface. The end of each stitch is worked in the same mesh opening as the one above or below it. Traditionally no spaces are left uncovered. Sturdiness and the simplicity of the design make bargello-stitched canvases suitable for upholstery, pillows, and seat cushions. Although either single-thread or penelope canvas in a wide range of sizes is most satisfactory, other balanced 50/50-weave fabrics are also useful. These are fabrics in which the warp and weft are equally visible: Duraback or monk's cloth, aida cloth, specially designed for counted thread stitchery, and pebble cloth or basket weaves in cotton, linen, wool, or mixed fibers. Softer fabrics require a stretched and taut surface to eliminate puckering, and should be fastened to a stretcher or tambour hoop. The cut edges can be protected from fraying by applying ¾″ masking tape all around, or by sewing the edges with an overcast stitch. Irregular shapes should be marked on a square or rectangular canvas but not cut out until the work has been completed. A generous margin of at least three inches should be left around the design area.

Many types of wool are suitable, particularly two-ply tapestry yarn and three-strand, two-ply Persian yarn. Three-strand Persian yarn can easily be separated and used singly or in multiples. The amount of Persian strands to be used is determined by the canvas mesh size. Larger sizes require heavy weights of yarn for complete coverage; finer meshes such as a No. 18 canvas can be easily covered with a single strand. A few stitches practiced on a corner of the canvas will indicate coverage density. Large canvas meshes may require three, four, or five strands of Persian yarn for certain stitches and different effects. Wools, cotton floss, and silk threads can be mixed for interesting textural effects. The fine detail of needlepoint can be combined with bargello stitches of broader scale for variation.

Use blunt tapestry needles with large eyes for canvas and more sharply pointed ones with long slender eyes for fabric. The correct needle will slip handily into the fabric spaces without splitting the warp or weft of the backing material. Most needle manufacturers identify needle sizes with numbers, the lower numbers indicating finer needles. Avoid confusion by looking at the needles as well as the numbers before making a selection. Threading the needle correctly is important. When two strands are called for, use one long strand doubled over to a final length of about eighteen inches. Short lengths are more practical. Fraying due to abrasion is bound to occur if yarn is worked through canvas again and again. Discard frayed sections. If the yarn is not doubled over, change the position of the needle on the thread frequently to avoid weakening the yarn in any one place. When many colors are used, work with several needles, each threaded with a different color.

View your yarn colors in daylight. Artificial light, either incandescent or fluorescent, is deceptive. Try to examine and compare a variety of colors at the same time. Never determine a choice based on a small sample or a single strand. Look at the colors in a mass held so that the light is not filtering through the strands. Yarns should be colorfast and preferably mothproofed.

Color choices are, of course, personal. A wide variety of tints and tones is available. Very subtle shading effects can be achieved by choosing a selection of graduated tints of a single color. Great depth can be achieved by applying sharply contrasting colors so that they appear to funnel back from a very light color uppermost to a very dark color in the background.

Bargello embroidery in an unbroken pattern line, an over-four under-two step progression of stitches, all of the same length but with a graduated number of stitches to each step. Worked on 14-mesh canvas in two-ply wool. Hanna Hale

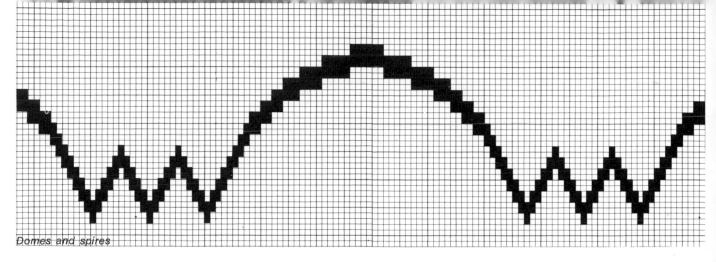

Domes and spires

Bargello embroidery in an unbroken flame pattern line, a variation on the preceding design. Notice the additional length of the curve due to the increased number of stitches in each step. Jan Silberstein

This pattern line is similar to those in the two preceding photographs, the difference being notably in the change of the curve's direction. After the unbroken pattern line has been established, each successive line follows the same course. Ruth Karlitz

Begin this pattern in the same manner as the unbroken line design in the preceding photograph. Work down to the sixth row and reverse the pattern. Complete the center. The pattern was worked in four shades of pink and white with a change from yarn to silk thread. Lillian Goldman

A zigzag pattern of sharp peaks done in short stitches. Lillian Goldman

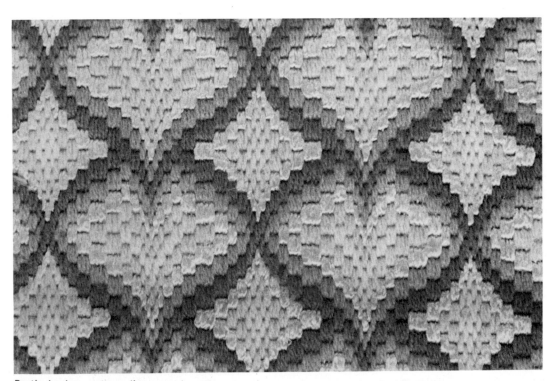

Partly broken pattern lines, each pattern forming a self-contained unit. All stitches are of the same length done over four threads and under two, stepping up and down. Worked in shades of pink in yarn and silk thread. Lillian Goldman

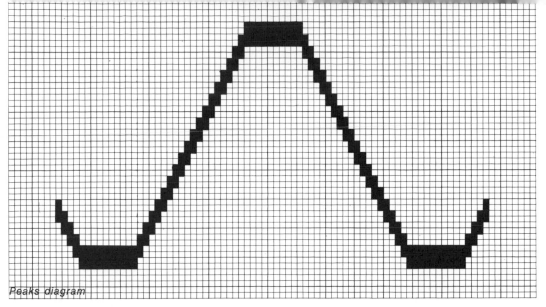

Peaks diagram

Above: Geometric plateaus in an unbroken pattern line, dipping and rising deeply in single strokes from a flat area of ten stitches. Ruth Karlitz

Below: Another flame pattern variation, rising and dipping from wide curves. Ronnie Schiller

Lighted flame design is a partly broken pattern. An illusion of great depth is produced by graduating tones of a single color from light to dark. Rosalie Adolf

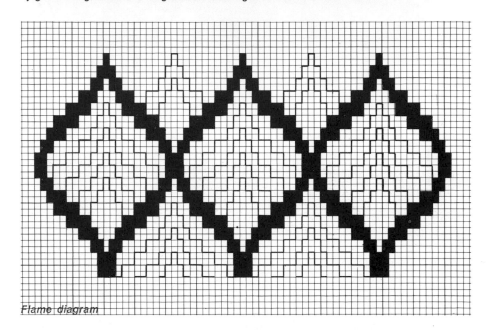

Flame diagram

Pattern similar to that in the preceding photograph but arranged in uncurved diamonds. Rosalie Adolf

Fully rounded curves are formed by gradually increasing the number of stitches at each step. Depth is achieved by using gentle gradations of color from light to dark. Ruth Karlitz

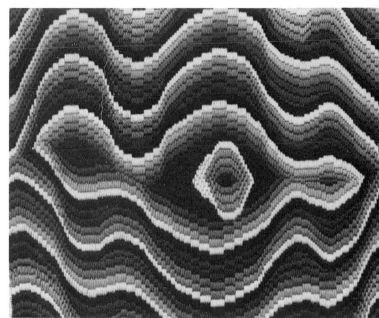

Asymmetrical free-form bargello pattern. Hanna Hale

Basketweave pattern worked in shades of red and blue with white. Beulah Friedman

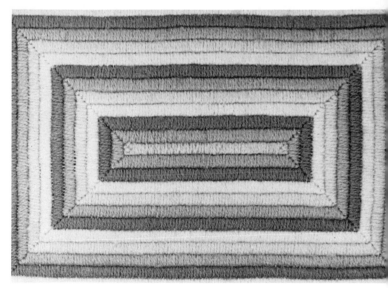

Simple straight stitches forming rectangles with mitered corners produce a pattern resembling corduroy. Subtle and unobtrusive, the corduroy pattern is an excellent foil for flamboyant bargello stitchery when used on the reverse side of pillows. Lillian Goldman

RADIAL BARGELLO

Depart from the traditional horizontality of needlepoint and bargello by devising radial patterns. Canvas mesh is equally spaced and can be worked in any direction. Start from a center point and work outward. Think of the canvas area as a square, or a circle within a square. Draw an X from corner to corner. Hold the canvas in the direction in which you are working, changing the direction with each quarter or segment of the design. Intricate designs can be achieved by drawing additional radial lines from the center to the perimeter. Plan your design on graph paper scaled in a size corresponding to the mesh of the canvas. Ten-mesh canvas corresponds to graph paper measuring ten squares to the inch. Draw the radiating lines from the exact center of the area to be covered, running diagonally through the corners of the squares. The two stitches on either side of the radial line will look like a mitered corner, the stitch running upward emerging from the same hole as the stitch running sideways.

Change of pace and change of texture are easily accomplished by combining areas of bargello and needlepoint. A central design worked in bargello in an undulating or irregular free form can be surrounded with needlepoint to finish the square or rectangle.

Methods for starting from the center:

A. Two bargello stitches next to each other run in each of four directions. The stitches that change the direction form a right angle and emerge from the same hole. The resulting small space at the center could be covered with a tent stitch.

B. Skip a space between the bargello stitches, covering the center space with a long cross-stitch.

C. Widen the space between the two starting bargello stitches appreciably, filling the center with needlepoint.

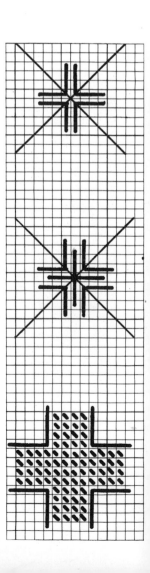

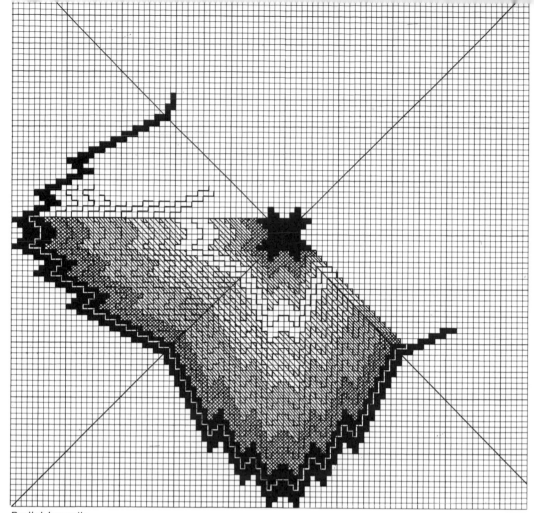

Radial bargello

Above: Diagram for four-way bargello design.
Left: Finished bargello worked in multiple shades of a single color against a needlepoint background.

Radial bargello with needlepoint background, designed and worked by the author.

DESIGNING

PART III

It has been said that the scope of art was enlarged when Matisse discovered Persian art and Picasso discovered African art. We live in a lively, affluent world of records, reproductions, and instant communication. Knowing craftsmen carefully study the work of the ancient and not-so-ancient worlds, of the Peruvians as well as the Victorians, of peasants as well as royalty. Examples of work by artisans of these periods are diagramed and documented in texts and museums and should be consulted, not for copying and repeating, but for study, for the redefinition and adaptation of old designs and techniques in new and personal ways, using contemporary materials.

There is no one way to design; no right way or wrong way. Just as there are many values of gray between black and white, so there are as many personal approaches to designing. To think is to have image-producing ideas, to see is to record design images, to dream is to rearrange these design images. The recesses of the mind are crisscrossed with ideas and images for designing, one radically different from another, others just a shade of gray away from the preceding ones. The problem is to select and discard, to clarify and pinpoint thought until a design image recurs and becomes uppermost in your mind. Then examine the image carefully without undue emotional or sentimental attachment.

People who love to make things usually collect and surround themselves with objects that stimulate speculation and feed the imagination. In the context of sufficient experience and background an idea may arrive in a sudden burst of inspiration. Most often, however, design ideas are triggered by a small amount of inspiration and resolved only with a vast amount of preparation. Crafts people spend part of their preparation in researching technique and materials. Of course, no matter how beautiful the craftsmanship, the finished result can only be as worthy as the basic design. Designs emanating from your own consciousness are personal and have creative potential. Occasionally images come into play that are inspired by admiration for other people's work. These should be recognized as what they are—merely a point of departure. All reference material existing in nature or reproduced photographically is a potential source of design.

In between the great periods in the development of art less important periods superseded each other in rapid succession. New design images have been derived, for instance, from the style known as Art Deco, developing during the lively period in art flourishing between the two World Wars. Unlike Art Nouveau with its turn-of-the-century rebellion against industrialization, Art Deco embraced the look of the machine product, combining it with the work of the artisan. The result was a new image of piercing zigzags and geometric shapes incorporated in the design of furniture, graphic art, fashions, jewelry, interiors, architecture, and machinery. Fabric design and ornamental stitchery reflected the highly distinctive design elements of this period, just as Oriental styles influenced design in Western Europe during the first half of the eighteenth century, changing the way common garden flowers were interpreted in decoration and embroidery.

In any art an intellectual accumulation of cultural knowledge, historical references, and artistic training is insufficient without the addition of an emotional human response to nature and the environment. In a society prizing scientific logic and productive thinking, so much has been said derisively about sentimentality that we tend to undervalue genuine sentiment. What is the specific quality inherent in a flower, for instance, causing the elusive reaction called admiration? Beauty, perhaps. Beauty by definition is a combination of qualities that delight the mind and the eye when we observe a shimmer of light, a sheaf of wheat, a brilliant butterfly, a swirl of hair, a field of daisies. Be aware of things you come upon by chance. Capture and preserve your reaction to instant movements, moments of great importance, a moment of grief, a very strange moment. Cherish a particular way of seeing; realize the inspiration inherent in moments of exuberance or despair. Evaluate the whites in a room, the cracks on a wall, an unusual relationship between objects and, as you design, make a statement of these relationships through the use of these basic elements:

LINE

A line may be active or passive, continuous or interrupted, thick or thin, or textured. Study the rhythm of the spider's web, the variety in rock or tree striations, the formation of every blade of grass and leaf grouping. The linear quality of street graffiti, the letters of the alphabet, newspaper engraving screens, television aerials, suspension bridges, the verticality of a skyscraper are equally valuable as a source of inspiration. An imaginative or dramatic approach will initiate an expressive line. Reinforce a single idea by reproducing it in multiples. Whole areas of design can be activated by variations on an original line.

Active line

Passive line

TEXTURE

So important to design are the visual aspects of texture and the physical sensations of touch that they must be considered from the start as a vital element of design. To a certain extent, a craftsman must take into

Thick and thin line

Textured line

Continuous line

Interrupted line

consideration the availability of desired materials. Where significantly textured materials are not easily secured creativity and ingenuity must come more fully into play. In literature a mental image of texture is created by description: smooth glass, gritty sand, velvety peaches, gossamer cobwebs. In stitchery, in addition to the use of differently structured and surfaced materials, try adding texture by knotting, shearing, braiding, brushing, plying, cutting, gathering, quilting, and trapunto.

FORM

When is a line not a line but a form? There is a natural continuity from one to the other. Where images intersect and touch, line plays a part. Line may develop naturally into form or form expend itself gradually into line. Cut a shape out of paper, hold it above drawing paper or a piece of fabric. Allow it to drift down and settle. Explore the possibility of depth by adding one form to another. Try this experiment with leaves, thinking only of the abstract images produced by their shapely contours. Arrange and rearrange them until the forms appear activated or passive in space. Carefully consider the space produced around the form. If the forms can be considered positive and the space around them negative, reverse the order, making the space positive and the original forms negative. Depending upon the subject matter, the effect will be of greater depth.

COMPOSITION

Just as color is a matter of personal taste, so is composition. Some artists may prefer certain geometric patterns which result in designs of perfect symmetry. Recognizing the value of rhythm and the harmony of close values, others prefer the variety offered by an asymmetrical composition. Traditional composition usually has a center of interest dominating the picture plane, supported by relevant, less important detail.

Working directly with the materials of the medium is still another approach to composition. Assemble the materials to be used and fully experience their unique qualities. Crush and move them about, feel the tex-

Exact placement affecting activity of form in space

tures, juxtapose the colors, fold and overlay them, to become creatively involved with the possibilities inherent in the medium and materials. The stitchery itself can be started with no preconceived ideas. Build a surface with thread as an artist does with paints. Your subject matter then becomes color, texture, and your own emotional responses rather than pictorial representation.

Some contemporary effects of great interest can be obtained by using reproduction techniques. Photostats are inexpensive and easy to obtain in urban areas. Sections of the art work can be enlarged and enlarged again in photostats to achieve a supergraphic effect, or can be reduced to minute size. Negative photostats may suggest new ideas, or the negative and positive photostats may be combined to vary or improve the basic design.

Notice the linear system used to transmit an image to the television screen. A screen must overlay a photograph to break the surface into a linear or dot pattern for transmission or reproduction. Several types of patterns are used: the circular screen, the horizontal or vertical screen, and the dots used in photoengravings for newspapers. Photoengraving screens range from superfine to very coarse. The most useful for enlarging are the coarser screens. Quilters and embroiderers will find these techniques for extracting the basic elements of a photograph easy to adapt to the needs of stitchery. A type of photographic image known as a dropped-out photograph is one in which the middle values are eliminated, leaving only the dark shadows to delineate the form. The dense forms remaining in a dropped-out photographic image are particularly suitable for appliqué work, in which only a highly stylized representation of an image is possible.

Many contemporary craftsmen are combining silk-screen and block-printing with stitchery. Batik, tie dyeing, and hand painting also work well with stitchery.

Depth

Without depth

With depth

COLOR

Color is a matter of personal taste. Be iconoclastic, break with stereotyped concepts. Try for spirited new combinations of color, of black and white, of natural earth colors, of the clear and translucent color so often characteristic of synthetic fiber. How many tints and tones of green exist in nature? Devise a similar monochromatic scheme using many tints and tones of a single color. A knowledge of color theories may be helpful in choosing combinations. The simplest way is to make a chart of the basic colors in order to study their relationships.

Red, yellow, and blue are called the primary colors. They cannot be made by mixing colors together. Before the use of chemical dyes, red and yellow came from the earth in the form of sienna and ocher, and blue was obtained from the indigo berry.

The secondary colors are made by mixing two primary colors together; for instance, blue and yellow produce green. A primary color combined with the secondary color next to it produces a tertiary or third set of colors, such as blue-green or yellow-green. Notice that colors placed next to each other on the chart are composed in part of a primary or secondary color and are related. Related colors look well together and are known as harmonious colors. Colors placed directly opposite each other on the color chart are known as complementary colors. Complementary colors of equal intensity are very strong, with a tendency to appear to vibrate when placed side by side. The nineteenth-century artists Van Gogh and Renoir frequently used the safe and still serviceable scheme of split complementary colors. Select a primary or secondary color, find its complement, and use the two colors on either side of the complement. For instance, red, yellow-green, and blue-green used in one-third proportions would be a split-complementary color scheme. A better relationship can be achieved by using more of the yellow-green and blue-green, which are harmonious because of their family relationship, with a small amount of the complement, red.

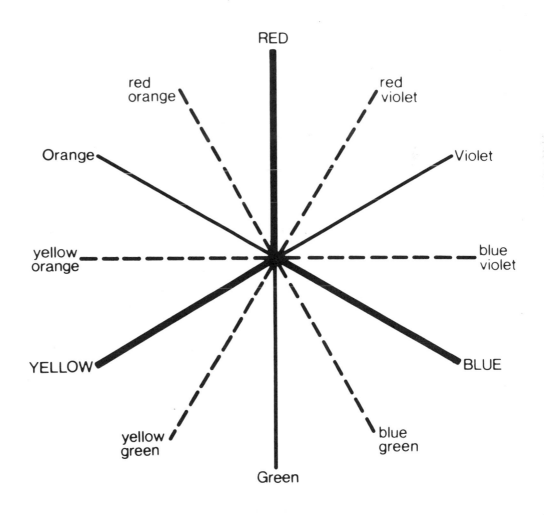

Color wheel

Observe the actual subject matter carefully. Use photographs as supplementary design material.

Reduce or enlarge a drawing or photograph by changing the scale with the aid of a grid drawn on an overlay of tracing paper. Enclose the entire design in a rectangle. Boxing of the subject matter should closely surround the form. Draw a diagonal line through the area from left to right, reaching from corner to corner and beyond. To reduce the size choose any point on the diagonal within the rectangle that will equal the width chosen for your design area. Draw a new horizontal line to the left and drop a new vertical line. For an increase in size, draw a new horizontal and vertical line from any point on the diagonal that extends beyond the corner. Divide the entire area of the original art work into halves, then quarters, and finally sixteenths. Complex designs can be broken into smaller segments for easier copying. Draw another grid system on a sheet of paper suited to the new width and depth of the stitchery design area. Transfer the outlines of the image from box to box.

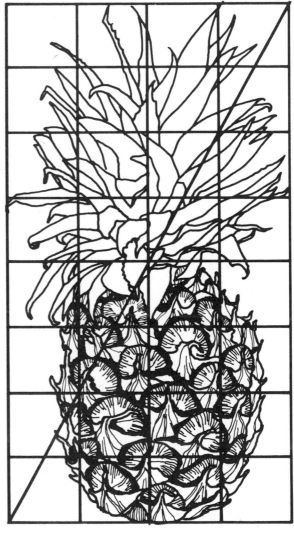

Drawing of the pineapple to scale.

Design for free stitchery and
appliqué leaf forms.

Design for satin stitch.

143

Design using both negative and positive views of areas of the image.

Star used as a symbol of the pineapple texture.

Above, left: Abstracting a photograph: Cut the entire photograph apart horizontally, in strips of graduated sizes and reassemble the pieces.

Above, right: An entirely new image made by cutting the photograph into concentric circles and rotating each section clockwise.

Right: Cut the photograph vertically into even strips and re-space the sections, causing horizontal distortion.

Familiar objects are often unobserved objects. Study the design possibilities in their characteristic stance, their uniquely individual contours and textures, and in their color arrangements.

Simplify the basic silhouette, using a soft pencil or pen and ink. Do not get lost in small detail. Delineate significant areas in black and white or positive and negative space. Add areas of texture. Place a tracing paper over this first sketch and make corrections and further adjustments on the overlay.

Use colored pencils or markers for color sketches. Try many arrangements, making a variety of thick and thin lines, reversing the negative and positive space, simplifying the basic shapes until the forms are pleasing and assume importance. Do not destroy the sketches; save them for comparison or to make revisions and new designs.

146

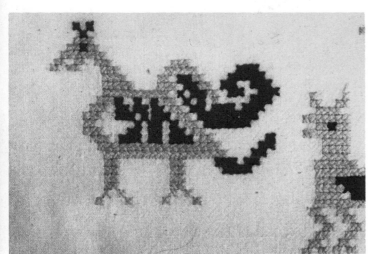

Mexican cross-stitch embroidery based on observation of a bird.
In counted thread cross-stitches the angular design is dictated
by the geometric shape of the stitches. Collection of the author

Above and top left and right: Details of a Mexican embroidery
freely drawn on muslin and embroidered in satin stitch in red
and black cotton floss. Collection of the author.

A turkey worked in reverse appliqué, from the San Blas Islands. Collection of the author.

YELLOW BANANAS

Super Graphics: Select a single idea, enlarging the most significant factor with a photostat. Cut a few paper frame mats with
openings of several dimensions and move them over the surface
of the photostat to see exactly how much can be eliminated
without losing the idea implicit in the image.

Trace the outline of a single leaf. Cut a paper pattern, a template, or several templates of reductions or enlargements. Draw
around their contours by grouping the templates formally, in
front of each other, behind one another, or in a graduated series
of sizes. Try an informal arrangement, asymmetrical or with
shapes scattered at random.

Winter scene design by Mary Christiansen, adapted from a
Christmas card and embroidered in split, chain, and satin stitch
on linen.

Formal arrangement of leaf forms in machine-stitched
appliqué. Courtesy Rose Krakauer

A House in Sea Cliff, Long Island by Martha Miller. Machine appliqué using patterned cotton fabrics.

Banner designed by Pat Tavenner. Silk-screen printed fabric appliquéd to a backing material. Art work silk-screened from a photograph is often used to make multiples for an edition of banners.

Upper: *Photograph prepared with a circle line conversion screen of the type used to reduce a photograph to a line engraving for newspaper reproduction. Line screen conversions of photographs can be obtained from local photostaters or printers. The line conversion is shown pinned in position over dressmakers' tracing paper and fabric, ready for transferring with a tracing wheel.*

Lower: Ms. Libby Liberty. *Embroidery in split stitch. Design by the author based on a screened photograph.*

Printed fabric is silhouetted and appliquéd to a backing in a banner designed by Pat Tavenner

Unfinished needlepoint screen by Harriet Pomerance, depicting an archeological site on Crete.

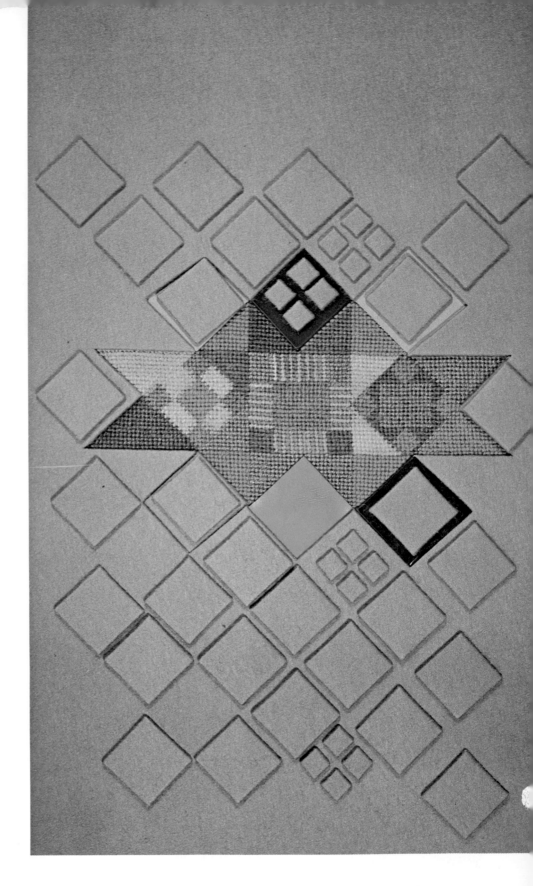

Diamonds *by Anne But-*
ler. Needlepoint on
canvas sewn to felt
background, surrounded
by additional felt and
leather diamond shapes.

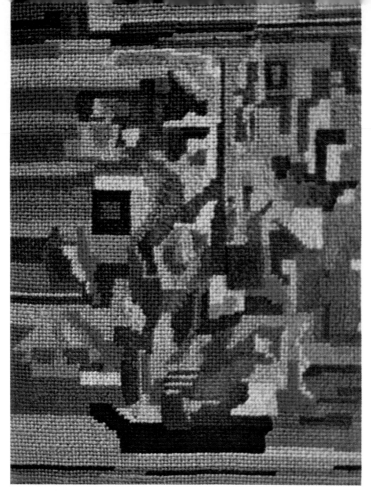

Above, left: Floral needlepoint by Shirley Silbert.

Above, right: Après Klee *by Harriet Pomerance, a 15″ roundel of needlepoint on stretched linen background.*

Left: The Gossipers *by Veronica Roth. Embroidery on natural linen.*

Stuffed 5′4″ patchwork roundel by Irma Kukka?jar? Sisal rope covered with mul? colored tricot tubing.

Phoenix by Shirley Marein. Batik on silk with stitchery detail.

Uncle Bob *by Alma Lesch. Contemporary appliqué and stitchery composition.* Collection Joseph Heil, New York City. Photo Ferdinand Boesch. Courtesy American Crafts Council

PATCHWORK QUILTING AND APPLIQUE

PART IV

Could Joseph's coat of many colors have been made of patchwork? Very likely. Spinning and weaving were in a very primitive state, and cloth was extremely precious. Although his father Jacob had prospered, the gift would have been sufficient to excite the envy of Joseph's many brothers. Patchwork is an ancient form with no real proof of origin; probably it was the work of all simple country peoples.

Differences in patchwork, quilting, and appliqué are distinct, but all consist of pieces of fabric sewn together, and the forms often overlap. The earliest known examples come from China and Egypt. The principle of trapping body warmth by layering cloth has long been known to the Chinese. Quilting forms small air pockets when the top fabric is sewn to the backing; multiple pockets form if a filling is sandwiched between the top and bottom layer, adding to the warmth. Insulation produced by layering was also well known among desert peoples whose experiences include extremes of climate, with days that are very hot preceding evenings marked by sharp drops in temperature. The Crusaders, carrying appliquéd banners, wore appliquéd tunics and acquired a knowledge of quilting from the Arabs of the Near East. Quilting was a very effective protection under chain mail. Quilted shirts brought back to Europe from the Near East by the Crusaders spread the use of the technique during the thirteenth and fourteenth centuries.

Development of block form from a single unit in a sixteenth-century orphrey (a border or part of an ecclesiastical vestment). Applied work, with a counterchanged pattern in red velvet and gold cloth, joined with cording. 3'11" × 7½". Courtesy Victoria and Albert Museum

Above: Contemporary Italian applied work by designer Lydia Di Roma. Silk shantung with machine satin stitch joining. Courtesy Rose Krakauer

Above, left: Italian Renaissance pilaster hangings. The appliquéd pieces are cut from contrasting silk and velvet fabrics and counterchanged. Cut edges are trimmed and joined with couched cording. During the Middle Ages applied work was a less expensive substitute for tapestry weaving and reflected the subject matter of tapestry hangings. These sixteenth-century designs were adapted from brocaded weavings. Each unit is 6'4" × 1'9". Courtesy Victoria and Albert Museum

Below, left: Pilaster hanging of linen and green satin applied work, couched with cording. The late sixteenth-century development of an undulating plant form with flowers and buds may have evolved from lace patterns or from the introduction of Eastern fabrics. 8'7½" × 1'10". Courtesy Victoria and Albert Museum

The piecing of fabric to form designs was practiced in Egypt at least a thousand years before the Christian era. Royalty and people of nobility traveled a great deal. Tents, floor cushions, and door and wall hangings of patchwork and appliqué were easy to transport and provided a background of comfort, beauty, and status. Egyptian design with its broad range of visual symbols, is clear and precise, monumental in scale, and visible from a great distance. These design forms have endured through centuries, influencing Greek and Roman art. The spread of the Roman Empire through Western Europe was another link connecting this continuing tradition with contemporary times.

Few written records remain from the Middle Ages and Early Renaissance; those that still exist have few references to appliqué and quilted textiles for domestic use. However, there are many references in European literature and inventories to quilted armour, which was in use until the implements of war became formidable, requiring a more effective defense. The English quilters of Durham and Northumberland, by passing basic patterns from mother to daughter, have traditionally developed many quilting design patterns now used universally. Some pattern names are self-explanatory; others have been altered through phonetic misinterpretation; still others are named after the source of inspiration. The very popular Princess Feather, from which many border and circle patterns derive, may have been adapted from the Prince of Wales's coat of arms. (The pattern was known during the fourteenth century as the Prince's Feather.) Until the twentieth century few written pattern books with references of any exactitude existed.

Although early banners, ecclesiastical vestments, and burial pieces were constructed by piecing and applying fabric to fabric, it is extremely difficult to determine the exact time or place patchwork, appliqué, and quilting started to be used one in conjunction with the other. Patchwork quilts, a distinct and recognizable art form, although born out of dire necessity, may be uniquely American. Settlers brought "bed furniture" consisting of quilts, bed curtains, and canopy ruffles to America on the *Mayflower*. During the long journey these items provided privacy and a degree of comfort on the planks that served as bunk beds from the time the Pilgrims dropped anchor in Plimoth harbor, late in November 1620, until the following spring when a stockade and rudimentary cabins were completed. Because the development and manufacture of cloth comprised a third of England's economy, skilled workers such as toolmakers and wheelwrights were not permitted to emigrate by law. So important was the work of the wheelwright in the construction of the spinning wheel that the hands of those apprehended attempting to leave as stowaways were chopped off as punishment and as an example to others. British colonial Navigation Acts prohibited the manufacture of cloth, compelled the settlers to supply England with raw materials, and mandated buying from England. The Acts were difficult to enforce; smuggling was rampant during this period, and some skilled workers did reach America. Until the settlers were secure and could produce a crop for exchange, clothing was patched and patched again. Every scrap of material was saved and used again in a new form. The Log Cabin quilt pattern of many one-inch strips of fabric was one of the earliest and most practical ways of using scraps.

Sailing ships brought cloth from Europe for trade with the Indians and for barter with the colonists. Surplus crops for barter were scant and cloth prices prohibitive. The scraps left over after the cutting of clothing were as valuable as the clothes themselves. These pieces, fitted together irregularly so that nothing was wasted, came to be known as Crazy Patch quilts. Later, when the need for them was less pressing, the Crazy Quilt idea was used to commemorate important events. A piece of fabric from a christening dress, a party dress, a uniform, or a wedding dress, saved and incorporated in a quilt, was a needlewoman's

Star of Bethlehem quilt of patchwork and appliqué. The star, as well as the border, is made of patchwork in early chintzes, English calicoes, and copperplate printed fabrics. Silhouetted floral bouquets are appliquéd to background fabric. Courtesy Shelburne Museum, Shelburne, Vermont

way of recording outstanding events occurring within a family. During the Victorian era a smaller, very elegant comforter was used in the parlor. Luxurious Crazy Quilts were assembled from silks and velvets, satins and brocades, and were heavily decorated with embroidered flowers and elaborate stitching.

The making of these piece-work quilts was often used as a learning experience for very young needleworkers. After skills were developed, a special pattern might be attempted, possibly the magnificent but difficult Star of Bethlehem. Many of these early quilts were more than ten feet square. Prior to the Revolutionary War, the bed, valued and treasured, placed importantly in what might be the only room in the house, was occupied by the entire family. A masterpiece quilt on an individual subject sometimes required quantities of special colors or patterns to complete. It was not uncommon for two quilts to be worked on simultaneously. The second quilt, made in a crazy patch pattern, absorbed the scraps left after cutting the special subject matter for the first, more prestigious patchwork.

All patchwork or pieced quilts are based on the basic geometric shapes: the square, the triangle, the rectangle, and the circle, cut and arranged in infinite combinations. Just as various are the many different names for these combinations, such as those based on only one of many pattern forms: the elegant Star of Bethlehem, the Blazing Star, California Star, Brunswick Star, Chained Star, Coffin Star, Dolly Madison Star, Diamond Star, Evening Star, Feathered Star, Flying Star, Friendship Star, Guiding Star, Harry's Star, Lucinda's Star, and the Le Moyne Star, often called Lemon Star. Others are the Liberty Star, Lone Star, Missouri Star, Pointed Star, Northumberland Star, Rising Star, Prairie Star, Rolling Star, Travel Star, Variable Star, Morning Star, Starry Path, Glittering Star, Potted Star, Martha Washington Star, Jackson's Star, Barbara Fritchie Star, Hexagon Star, and many, many others. Regional and commemorative names are given to the same or similar patterns having slight variations, and in addition there are differences in personal interpretation for the popular star form, inspiring more descriptive titles.

Above: American patchwork, particularly the Log Cabin pattern, is a tribute to the creativity, thrift, and pragmatism of its makers. Collection of the author

Below: Appliqué quilt design sold by the Paragon Company during the American folk art revival period in the 1940s. The Calico Rose pattern is a derivation of the early nineteenth-century Persian Palm lily design. Worked by the author as a young girl.

Above: Early nineteenth-century quilted patch-work. Block arrangements of squares and tri-angles. Collection Mr. and Mrs. Sydney Jacoff

Above, right: English patchwork quilt with feather border, in silk, satin, and velvet; mid-nineteenth century. Courtesy Victoria and Albert Museum

Right: Victorian crazy quilt of velvet, silk, and satin brocade with silk floral embroidery and decorative embroidered elements joining each piece. Collection Mr. and Mrs. Sydney Jacoff

Late nineteenth-century American pineapple pattern patchwork quilt *cut from printed cotton fabric.* Courtesy Victoria and Albert Museum

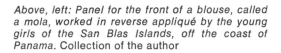

Above, left: Panel for the front of a blouse, called a mola, worked in reverse appliqué by the young girls of the San Blas Islands, off the coast of Panama. Collection of the author

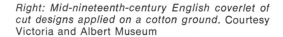

Right: Mid-nineteenth-century English coverlet of cut designs applied on a cotton ground. Courtesy Victoria and Albert Museum

Garden flowers are as popular a subject in appliqué as the star is in pieced patchwork. Appliqué, requiring little of the mathematical precision necessary in patchwork, is less pure and more romantic, lending itself to curvilinear forms, variety in medium, and additional adornment. Early appliqué examples were often worked around a central floral medallion surrounded by wreaths, leaves, and vines. Some examples have additional birds, ribbons, and fruit, many decorated with embroidery for emphasis, and most are quilted. Friendship quilts, made by groups of people, commemorated events and were bestowed as gifts. It is significant that the eighteenth and nineteenth centuries and the early part of the twentieth century reflect involvement, interest, love, friendship, and *esprit de corps,* often under adverse conditions. With the exception of the somber work of the Shaker people, the patchwork and appliqué quilts communicate a joyous feeling for color, emotional and personal expression, and a great sense of pleasure and pride in craftsmanship.

Lack of rigidity, the ability to develop a design emotionally and freely without restriction, to build, to add, and to rearrange, have made appliqué an extraordinary medium for wall hangings today.

166

Appliquéd and embroidered wall hanging from India. The border is inset with small mirrors. Courtesy Sona The Golden One

All Seasons Altar Frontal *by Beryl Dean. Patchwork in many fabrics, including cloth of gold and velvet with colored metallic embroidery.* Chapel of the Westminster Hospital, London

Study in Light and Shadow *by Doris Hoover. Patchwork of linen, cotton, and velveteen machine tucks, pleats, and gathers with covered buttons.* Collection Mr. and Mrs. Everett Berg. Photo Howard Fisher

PATCH-WORK

GLOSSARY

PATCHWORK
Small geometric pieces of fabric, cut and sewn together to form a totally new surface.

TEMPLATES
Shaped guides cut from cardboard, plastic, or metal for tracing on paper or fabric.

BLOCK
One complete design unit of individual patchwork pieces.

CRAZY QUILT
Random arrangement of irregular scraps of material, sewn to form a totally new surface.

BASTING/TACKING
Temporary stitches holding patterns and fabric in place.

JOINING
Seaming of patchwork pieces and block units.

BACKING
Fabric foundation for patches. Certain patterns, particularly Log Cabin and Crazy Quilt, require construction directly on a backing fabric in addition to a bottom layer of fabric to hold padding or serve as lining.

Patchwork has endured for centuries as a craft. Although thrift is partly accountable for its survival, a love of color and variety, and an everlasting interest in puzzles, both play a part. Patchwork can be a mathematical challenge. Special equipment is unnecessary; just the usual contents of the home sewing box suffice: needles, pins, scissors, thread, thimble, and a stiff substance to make templates for geometric patterns. The fabric may be scraps saved from other sewing projects or those specially purchased. If the patchwork is to be functional and sustain wash and wear, the fabrics used should all wear equally well. Percale, broadcloth, muslin, or any other closely woven material that does not fray will be suitable. Avoid flimsy, easily stretched, or nubby fabrics. Fabrics of man-made fibers such as rayon or nylon often fray easily and are difficult to work with.

Geometric patterns should be cut with exacting care. Cut with the warp and the weft at right angles to the pattern; otherwise the pieces will not lie flat. The most popular shapes are the square, rectangle, diamond, and hexagon because they can be pieced together without the addition of other shapes. These are known as one-patch designs. Seemingly easy, the one-patch design requires the ability to visualize the project in its entirety, considering color relationships and the way color affects the apparent formation of the patterns. The one-patch pattern is most often worked from the center toward the outside of the piece, sometimes utilizing a medallion center or a border formed from contrasting colors. Cutting the individual pattern square or rectangle diagonally in half increases the possibilities of variety in color and pattern arrangement in a two-patch design. These arrangements, cut in contrasting colors, are laid out in six-, eight-, ten-, or twelve-inch square blocks. After a suitable amount of blocks has been sewed, the finished blocks are joined to form a larger surface. Early geometric designs are based on the wide variety of possibilities produced by folding a square of cloth. Most of the pattern designs for pieced patchwork are called four- or nine-patch, four being the square of two, and nine the square of three, indicating that the patches are laid out two squares down and two squares across or three squares down and three across.

CONSTRUCTING PATCHWORK TEMPLATES

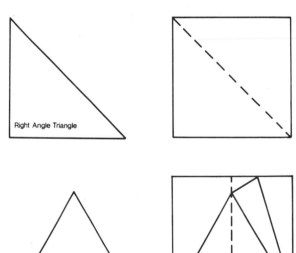

Right Angle Triangle

Equilateral Triangle

TEMPLATES

Apart from Crazy Quilts, which can be made from irregular pieces of any size, most patchwork requires the use of templates to keep all the cut pieces the same size and shape. Many types of templates are on the market in a variety of sizes and shapes, but you can easily make your own templates of cardboard or plastic. Heavy-weight clear acetate is good to use because it can be placed over a printed fabric and moved about like a window to select a desired section of the printed design. Score the acetate with a sharp blade or knife. Snap off the excess by pressing it down against the edge of a table. Cardboard templates are excellent but may need replacement after extensive use.

For accuracy, it is necessary to have two templates, one the actual size of the piece to be cut, and the other with a ¼″ seam allowance. If the patchwork is to be machine sewn, trace around the larger template and cut out the piece. One or two pieces may be cut at one time, but inaccuracies can occur if many are cut at once. Center the smaller template within the larger one to trace a sewing guideline.

Hand sewing requires a slightly different approach. Cut the fabric from the larger template, including the seam allowance. The smaller template is then used to cut paper templates called paper patches to serve as guides for turning in the seam allowances accurately. Cut the paper patches from brown wrapping paper or any other medium-weight paper. Avoid a glossy-surfaced stock. Pin the paper to the wrong side of the fabric, centering it with care. Turn and baste the seam allowance over the paper patch. Use a long running stitch. There is no need to knot the finished basting thread; removal will be easier after all the pieces are joined if it is left loose. Holding the right sides together, join the patchwork pieces by overcasting the edges with matching thread. Use fine but firm stitching, with as little as possible showing on the right side. Proceed from one patch to another, taking special care that all the points come together. Some folding and unfolding for adjustment may be necessary. Remove the basting thread and press pieces on the wrong side. Remove the patch papers. If the papers are caught in the overcasting, pull them gently, allowing the thread to cut through the paper. Work in convenient blocks or sections, storing the finished pieces in plastic bags until you are ready to assemble them. If the final shape is to be square or rectangular, zigzag or uneven edges must be filled with half or part pieces. The alternative is to trim the finished patchwork to size. Patchwork used for quilts, coverlets, or wall hangings may be interlined or padded, then backed with a plain or matching fabric. To keep the padding from shifting, tie padded patchwork quilts with knotting at intervals, or sew them with a running stitch around the blocks or in an over-all quilting pattern.

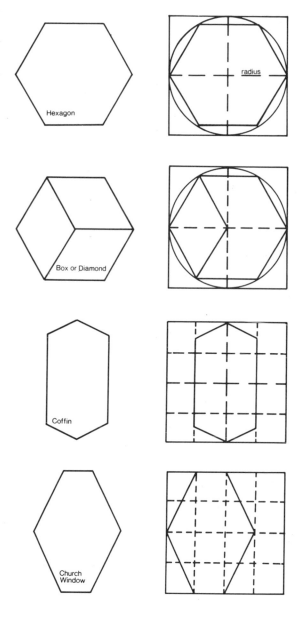

LOG CABIN PATTERN

Very old, very American, this pattern is still vitally pertinent to the contemporary craftsman interested in optical illusions and the illusion of deep space. Depth is controlled by a careful choice of tonal values and by the number of steps used in receding toward the central square.

1. A backing foundation must be used for each block of Log Cabin strips. Cut an 8″ square of thick cardboard for a foundation template.

2. Rule guidelines on the template in order to measure cabin strips against it. Include three or more steps plus the center square. The first strip is marked one width longer than the central square. Each succeeding strip is marked two widths longer than the first strip.

3. Using the template, cut out as many 8″ squares as will be needed for the backing foundation. Allow ¼″ extra all around for joining the squares.

4. Cut strips 1″ wide, including a ⅛″ seam allowance on either side, or cut wider strips 1¼″ in width, including seam allowance. The length will vary from short to long, according to the measurements on the cardboard template.

5. Using a white pencil, run a visible line diagonally from corner to corner of the cloth square, crossing in the center.

6. Center a small square of fabric on the crossed line. Baste the square to the background, leaving ⅛″ seam allowance.

7. Pin the shortest strip to the bottom center of the square, wrong side facing out, extra length projecting at the left. Sew the strip to the background, stitching within seam allowances of the center piece. Do not sew the extra length; just cover one side of the center square, stitching ⅛″ in from the edge. Fold over and away from the center. Press down.

8. Sew a second strip along the right side, overlapping the bottom strip. Fold over and away from the center. Press down.

9. Place the third and fourth strip around the square in the same manner.

172

10. Tuck the fourth strip under the first strip at the bottom. Lift up the extra length of the bottom strip and continue sewing across the fourth strip. Complete additional rows until the foundation material is covered, forming a complete block. Join the blocks.

11. Splitting the color distribution diagonally: the upper portion in darker tones, the lower portion in light tints of color. The design of the entire quilt or cover must be considered when splitting the blocks tonally. The placement of the blocks themselves will then form another pattern.

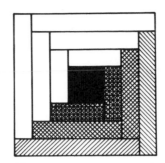

11

BABY BLOCKS PATTERN

Baby Blocks, Tumbling Blocks, or plain Boxes, is a three-dimensional optical illusion pattern made by dividing a single hexagon into three diamonds. The three diamonds must be cut from distinctly different tones or patterns to be effective. Maintain the illusion by always placing the darkest piece on the same side of the hexagon and the lightest piece at the top.

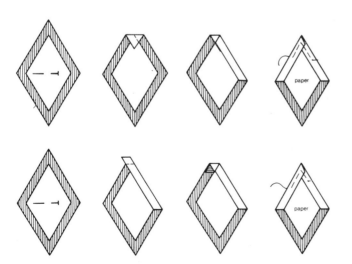

TWO WAYS TO FOLD UNDER THE SHARP CORNERS OF A DIAMOND PATCH AROUND A PAPER TEMPLATE

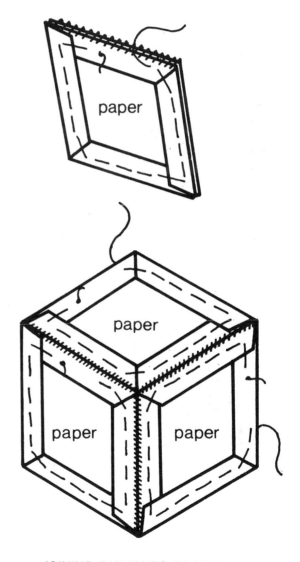

JOINING DIAMONDS TOGETHER TO FORM A BABY BLOCK

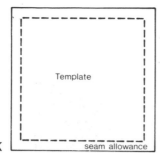

PUFF PATCHWORK

Template

seam allowance

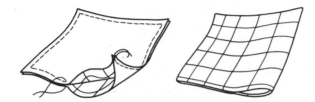

DESIGN COMBINATIONS FOR PUFF PATCHWORK

CHECKERBOARD

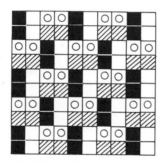

RECTANGLES

ZIGZAGS

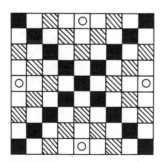

CROSS

PUFF PATCHWORK IN SQUARES

Contemporary patchworkers are ingenious in devising assembly-line techniques for speeding up traditionally lengthy processes. Puff patchwork in squares combines design, padding, and backing in one step. Designing is based on the probable combinations of square multiples. Squares can be alternated for a checkerboard effect, grouped in rectangles for a laid-brick pattern, or to make stripes, variations on a cross, or random color arrangements. Sketch the design on graph paper with colored pencils or felt-tipped markers in order to determine both the effect of the design and the amount of fabric necessary. Work with a 4½″ square for what will be a full 4″ square after the padding is inserted. Cut two cardboard templates, one 4½″ square, the other 5″ square including the seam allowance. Use the larger template to cut out the fabric, the smaller one for outlining the sewing guideline inside the seam allowance. Before cutting the fabric, line up the warp and weft at right angles by drawing a thread out and cutting along the drawn line. Place the cardboard template in line with the weft (sometimes called the crosswise grain) to keep the patchwork square flat. If a fiber batting is used for padding, cut a 4″ cardboard template for this. Hold the template to the padding material and cut around it with a scissors.

Place the top and bottom square patches, right sides together, for hand sewing or machine stitching around three sides along the seam allowance. Turn the sewn patches inside out, carefully pushing the corners out, insert the interlining, fold in the seam allowance, and slip-stitch the edges together.

Arrange the completed squares according to your graph-paper design and join the patches. Finish the edges of the quilt or pillow in any simple straightforward manner. You might topstitch all around the edges with two rows of small, even running stitches, each row ¼″ away from the other, or bind the edges with a matching or contrasting piping.

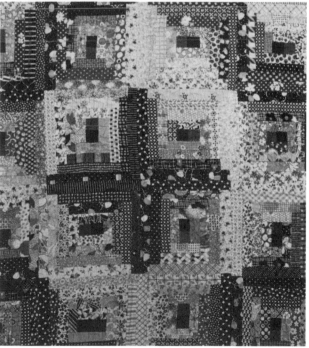

Above: Puff Patchwork squares arranged in blocks ready for joining. Courtesy Phyllis Floyd

Above, left: Baby Blocks in contrasting patterns.

Below, left: Detail of contemporary American Log Cabin Patchwork quilt. Collection Pat Newman

QUILT-ING

GLOSSARY

QUILTING
A spaced pattern sewn over an entire surface, joining top and bottom materials to prevent shifting. Used with or without a padded interlining.

TIED QUILTING
Layered materials fastened at intervals with knots, with or without interlining.

TRAPUNTO
Raised, embossed effect produced by stuffing specific design areas that have been outlined by sewing through layered materials.

The "fabric sandwich," as quilting has been called, has no recorded beginning, and its popularity will in all probability continue endlessly. Utilitarian, sensible, practical, and decorative, the form has touched everyone and everything in every century. It has been used to make clothing, bedding (including matresses), upholstery, insulation, toys, packing and building materials, and to enhance the appearance of accessories and wall hangings. Of course, such wide and diverse usage necessitates similarly divergent materials for the purpose of fabrication. Cotton, wool, linen, silks, and velvets are traditional materials, in addition to many combinations, such as today's man-made fibers, and linsey-woolsey, a coarse fabric much used in earlier centuries, composed of a linen warp filled with a wool weft. Padding, stuffing, batting, or interlining materials range from the early use of corn husks and paper to contemporary cellulose products.

Taut, even stretching is essential when quilting several layers of material. Self-supporting frames for quilting are commercially available for purchase, but a frame is easy to construct. Four straight pieces of lumber cut to assemble into a rectangular form are all that is necessary. Support can be provided by the backs of chairs, or by laying the frame counter to counter, or by using saw horses. Choose lumber in a weight suitable to its length. On long lengths lumber that is too thin will bend or sag in the middle. The longer sides of the rectangle, called runners, are usually long enough to take the full length of the work, and may be flat rails, round poles, or faceted moldings. In order to wind or roll the layers of fabric to be quilted, the runners and stretchers must be held firmly in place with a removable nut and bolt. Flat lumber can be held with a C clamp. On a commercial frame these

Rare six-pointed Evening Star design of fully pieced patchwork surrounded by hexagons in a late nineteenth-century quilt, probably of Pennsylvania Dutch origin. Patterned in orange and white and solid orange calico. Collection of the author

runners are fitted through the supporting stand and turn within a ratchet device to roll the work and tighten the tension. The side stretcher lengths are shorter. It is assumed that the size of the frame will be such that two workers, sitting one on either side, will be able to reach the center comfortably for easy stitching.

Many quilters working in a small area may prefer a large (tambour) double-ring embroidery frame with an adjustable ratchet. The adjustable ratchet expands the size of the outer ring to accommodate the layers of fabric. The work is done in small areas, moving the embroidery frame as needed. When quilting is not in progress, the material is removed from the hoops to relax the fabric and the threads.

Artists' canvas stretchers are also suitable for quilting. Attach the project to the stretcher with thumbtacks. Remove the thumbtacks and reposition the work as often as necessary.

It is possible to quilt small sections held in the hand by working one block at a time and

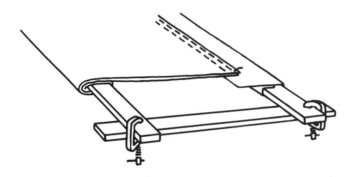

Prepare the long runner sides of the quilting frame with long strips of sturdy muslin or duck fabric about 9″ wide. Staple or attach the strips to each runner with short round-headed rug nails. Wrap the muslin once around each runner, allowing a flap of fabric to extend beyond the runner. Baste backing fabric to these strips with double rows of stitches. Spread the runners and the backing out on the floor or table and smooth the backing flat, add padding and top fabric and baste. Carefully roll the runners and fabrics in toward each other until a comfortable working area of about 3′ remains. Attach the runners to the side stretchers.

joining the blocks when all are completed. However, matching the quilting pattern during joining is painstaking and requires extra care.

Prepare for quilting on noncommercial frames by basting together the top, padding, and backing of the quilt on a table or flat surface. Start from the center and baste a large X across the entire surface, working from the center to the outside corners. Determine the pattern or form the quilting will take, remembering that the fundamental purpose is to join the layers of fabric. Traditional patterns are geometric outlines, fruit and flowers, feather scrolls, medallions, sea shells, and other free-flowing or representative forms. Patchwork quilting patterns more often follow the form of the cut pieces. Draw your designs on tracing paper or vellum. Transfer them to the fabric with a tracing wheel and dressmakers' tracing paper, or transfer a simple design to a piece of cardboard. Cut a cardboard template, place it on the fabric, and trace around the form with pencil or a chalk pencil. Sew with small, even running stitches, stabbing the needle up and down, the hand above the fabric passing the needle and thread down to the hand below. Several stitches can be taken horizontally on the needle at once, but the stabbing-up-and-down method is firm and more accurate, particularly for turning corners or working complicated curves.

TIED QUILTING

Tied quilting is a simple way to quilt, especially without a frame. Using a large-eyed needle, pull a cord or piece of yarn down through the layered materials from the front to the back and bring it up to the front again. Tie the two ends in a square knot on the front surface. The ends may be trimmed short or left long. A neat, tailored surface can be made by embroidering with French knots, taking one, two, or three turns around the needle according to the fullness desired, then returning the thread to the back of the bottom layer of fabric. Tie the two ends of the thread together on the back in a square knot and cut them short. As decora-

Tied quilting. Top, padding, and backing are tied with French knots spaced at regular or design intervals.

tion, and to make the work more secure, buttons and beads can also be used on the top surface, with the thread pulled through to the wrong side and the two ends knotted together. Before starting the tying, indicate the positions of the knots with a pencil. Pin large surfaces together and baste diagonal lines through all layers from corner to corner, crossing in the center, making a large X, or make a cross and divide each square again for more security. This is necessary to keep the layers of fabric from slipping. Commence knotting following a grid or other design pattern.

TRAPUNTO

Trapunto, a stitchery technique used to produce an effect of embossing, is sometimes known as cord quilting or stuffed quilting. It is important to use a stretcher to sew the outlines of large flat surfaces with narrow design areas. After the tension has been released, the narrow areas will be easier to fill. Choose a closely woven fabric for the top layer and a loose open-weave material such as scrim or gauze for the bottom layer. Arrange the layers of material with the bottom surface on top. Transfer the design to this bottom surface. Sew with a fine but firm running or back stitch, or machine sew around the design outlines.

Stuffed quilting is prepared in the same manner, varying the widths of the design areas. Many possibilities for original ideas are feasible when loose stuffing is used. Polyester fiber filling is most satisfactory and infinitely easier to work than cotton batting. A great variety of surface fabrics are interesting, but an open gauze weave backing is best; its threads are easily parted or cut in order to push or lay in soft batting. Use a slender stick to fill small corners properly. Do not overstuff; the pattern should be firm and distinct on the right side, but not distorted. After stuffing, sew the parted gauze threads together with a lacing or loose overcasting stitch. Combine cord quilting and stuffed quilting for a thick-and-thin effect. Use a backing fabric to cover the gauze layer.

Completed quilts and wall hangings are usually finished with a firm edge which may be made in several ways:

1. Turn in the edges and finish with a double row of running stitches.
2. Turn in the edges and insert a self- or contrasting piping.
3. Bind the edges with bias-cut self- or contrasting strips of fabric.
Sew by hand or use a sewing machine, but be consistent in the method you use on any item.

Narrow linear design outlines meant for cord quilting should match the width of the cord. To insert the padding, thread a blunt needle with a large eye with the cord. Make a slit in the gauze bottom surface, between the sewed outlines. Draw the cord through the stitched channel, bringing the needle up every so often, re-entering in the same hole after pulling the cord through. To prevent puckering, do not pull the cord tightly at each stop. Allow a small amount of extra cord to remain outside the exit hole each time the needle re-enters. Do not work with a too long cord; cut it and start again at intersections or turns in the design. Cord quilting requires a protective backing which is added after the quilting is done.

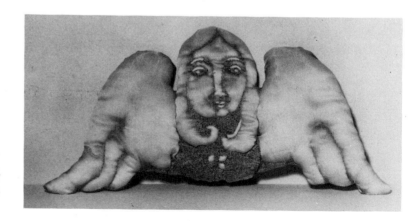

Above, and opposite, above: Trapunto pillows by Elsa Brown. Dacron semisheer fabric stuffed with polyester batting. Photos K. Y. Fung

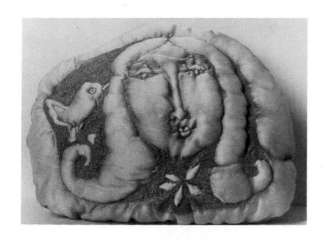

Place two layers of fabric together. Pin or baste with long running stitches to hold the fabric in place. Stitch the design freely on the right side, through the two layers of fabric, using a sewing machine darning stitch. Fill some areas with stitching texture by moving the fabric back and forth under the needle. Areas to be stuffed are slit on the wrong side, through the backing layer only, and filled with polyester fiber. Sew the slits together. Prepare a pillow backing. Pin the pillow top and the backing together, right sides facing each other. Sew together, leaving an opening for turning. Turn right side out and stuff with polyester fiber. Sew the opening, or insert a zipper closing before stuffing.

The features and detail are freely stitched on the right side of two layers of voile with machine darning. The fabric is moved freely under the needle until all surfaces not to be stuffed are covered with stitching. Slit the areas to be stuffed on the wrong side with small pointed embroidery scissors. Push the stuffing into place with a thin stick. To fill the narrow lines of the hair, thread a blunt needle with thick fluffy yarn and pull it through a small slit cut across the width between outlines. In a three-dimensional object, the back and sides are worked individually according to the design concept, in the same manner as the front. Place the right sides together and stitch all around except for an opening on an inconspicuous side. Turn right side out, stuff the interior, and sew the opening together.

Left: Beatrice *by Elsa Brown. Three-dimensional figure of Dacron and cotton voile padded with polyester fiber in the trapunto technique.* Photo K. Y. Fung

Springtide. *Detail of quilting by Nancy Friedman.*

In and Around *by Norma Minkowitz. Trapunto-padded, hand-woven form, with stitchery and crocheting.* Photo Kobler/Dyer Studios

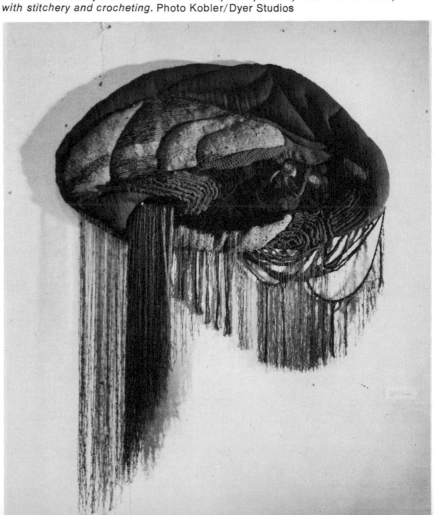

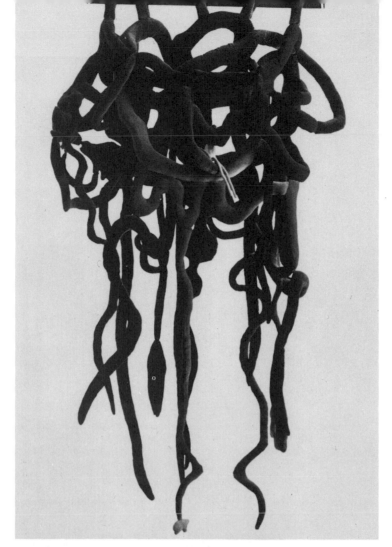

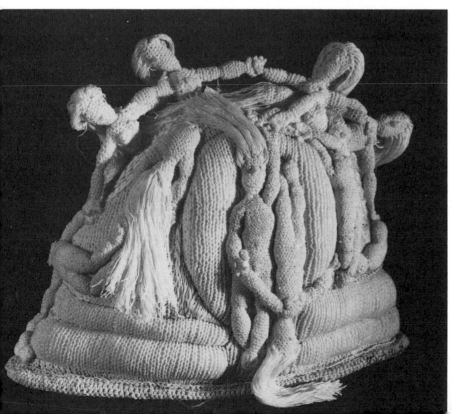

To the Honour of Spring *by Agneta Flock. Three-dimensional form of sewed and stuffed velvet with some patchwork.* Photo Bengt Widell

Left: For Women Only *by Norma Minkowitz. Three-dimensional construction of knitted fabric in trapunto with additional stitchery and crochet work.* Collection Mrs. Kenneth Hall. Photo Kobler/Dyer Studios

183

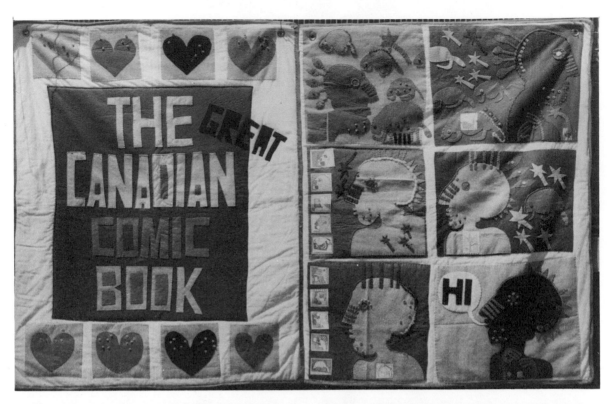

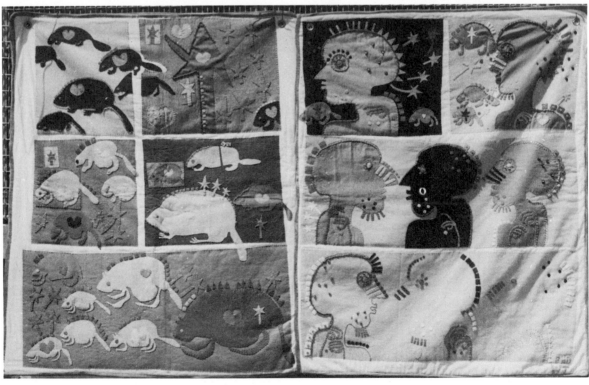

Great Canadian Comic Book *by Wendy Toogood. Cotton, felt, ribbon, and embroidery on cotton backing form flexible pages.* Photo Don Mabie

APPLI-QUE

GLOSSARY

APPLIQUÉ
Any materials cut and affixed to a background; and spaced next to each other or one over the other.

REVERSE APPLIQUÉ
The cutting away of one layer of fabric in specific design areas to expose another layer of fabric underneath. Also known as inlay or découpé.

BLIND STITCHING
Barely visible, concealed hemming stitches.

Maximum freedom of expression can be achieved by using appliqué as a collage technique. Any subject is possible, any medium or combination of mediums; fibers, fabrics, paper, vinyl, metal, leather, glass, or plastics, in any weight or dimension, are all suitable. Almost any material can be applied to a background by sewing, pasting, or bonding. The basic stitches required are easy; a running stitch or a blind hemming stitch suffices. Embroidery, either simple or elaborate, can be added, used for its linear quality, to change whole color fields, or to add texture. Probably the only difficult technical accomplishment involved is learning how to turn in an inverse point, such as those that occur at the intersections of scallops or on the outgoing points at the ends of stars. Many materials require turning under; others do not. Many finishes are attractive without neatly turned edges.

Art work attains significance through the individual differences evidenced in its execution. Your memory is a veritable warehouse of ideas, stored up by a lifetime of experience and education and influenced by personality, heredity, and physiological characteristics. Value your personal uniqueness. Value your own ideas. Designing for appliqué can be a great personal experience. The range of possibilities is vast, from Spartan minimalism to the contemporary popularity of memorabilia. Design directly with your materials, arranging and rearranging them on a suitable background.

Of course this method requires a large selection of materials at hand. Work from a sketch either drawn or made of cut paper. Large forms for experimental placement can be cut from newspaper. These paper sketches can be used as pattern pieces for cutting the final materials. Do not forget to add from ⅛″ to ½″ of extra fabric around the form as an allowance for hemming. Certain fabrics, such as velvet and others that tend to fray badly, require a larger hem allowance. Clip the seam allowance at short intervals to facilitate turning and easing around curves. Press the seam allowance to the wrong side with your fingernail, then pin the fabric to the background and baste it down. Blind-stitch around the edges, picking up a moderate amount of background fabric and as little fabric as possible from the applied piece so as to make the stitching practically invisible. Often it is also desirable to use a running stitch on the surface, 1/16″ in from the finished edge, as an aid in keeping the applied piece flat. Additional running stitches could be used to add a linear decorative pattern.

Silhouette of cut appliqué lettering showing seam allowance.

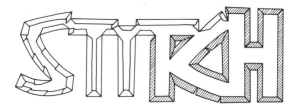

Reverse side showing slashing and folding necessary for turning under seam allowance.

MACHINE STITCHING

The sewing machine is a wonderful tool with untold design resources, a great inventive potential waiting to be expressed in a whole new vocabulary of stitches that are not better or worse than hand stitchery, but different. Explore the functions of all the attachments and levers and make full use of each technique for itself. Machine appliqué fabric to a background with an open zigzag stitch. A turned-under hem allowance is not always necessary if you sew by machine, particularly on heavy or close-woven fabrics. A close machine zig-

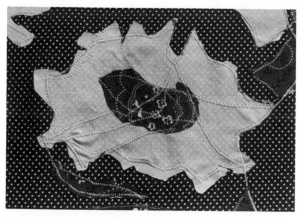

Spring Bouquet by Martha Miller. Detail showing free zigzag machine sewing.

zag stitch resembles satin stitch and produces a firm, durable finish. Run the stitches at right angles to the fabric. Around corners and curves, lift the presser foot often, turning the fabric slightly each time. The stitching can match the fabric or be of a contrasting color.

Free stitchery on the sewing machine is very exciting. The needle can be moved about like a pencil. Added color and variety can be achieved by switching to different threads in the bobbins. Sturdy fabrics such as duck and denim have less tendency to pucker than thin transparent fabrics which should be backed with paper or used double to eliminate undue puckering as the material moves through the machine. Place the material in an embroidery hoop, cover the feed plate, and remove the presser foot so that the fabric can be pushed back and forth freely under the needle. Altering the tension varies the stitch. Use the machine for couching, for overlaying net, gauzes, and organdies on the background fabric. Do not lose sight of the freedom and spontaneity inherent in machine embroidery. Try not to harness the fluidity that can be achieved with a free-flowing line. Think of it not as a means of imitating hand embroidery, but as a device that opens up a whole new range of possibilities in color, texture, and form.

REVERSE APPLIQUÉ

Reverse appliqué, as the name implies, is the opposite of traditional appliqué. It is a method of cutting away surfaces to expose those underneath rather than applying one layer of material to another. Felt, leather, or canvas, for instance, are nonfraying and can be bonded with adhesives. Of the fabrics that require hemming, lightweight, firmly woven fabrics are less difficult to work with than stiff heavy ones. Percales are the most useful.

The Cuna Indians of the San Blas Islands off the Atlantic coast of Panama are the most celebrated workers in the reverse appliqué technique, but the craft was also practiced by the early Egyptians and some African tribes. The work of the Cunas is highly prized by collectors because of their charmingly naïve approach to

Three-color reverse appliqué, basted in position. Curves were slashed and turned under before blind stitching.

design. Their work sometimes inadvertently bears a relationship to Pop Art. The island women reproduce in reverse appliqué a wide variety of subject matter common to their daily lives, including reproductions of the graphics printed on debris left by tourists, such as candy wrappers and empty cigarette packages. Their "molas," made of front and back panels executed in reverse appliqué and sewn together to form a blouse, are a precise and traditional art form existing within the culture of this protected group.

In reverse appliqué several contrasting colors of cotton fabric are stacked one on top of another, with parts of the top layers cut out to expose the colors of the layers beneath. The design becomes apparent as its individual elements are cut away and removed. The raw edges of the successive layers are hemmed under. More than three layers of fabric are difficult to handle, therefore small pieces of fabric are inserted in specific areas between layers to add more colors. Often the small cutout pieces that have been removed are used later as appliqué. Although the cuts are slender and the outlines can be made to move fluidly, embroidery is sometimes used to define further the form and to add to the surface texture.

Lion. *Cut and pasted appliqué of felt and wool on burlap by Eve Waldron, aged nine.*

Above: Ceiling in Flight *by Pat Tavenner. Hanging of silk-screened and stitched triangular forms.*

Right: Soft Parcheesi Board *by Sas Colby. Multicolored patchwork.*

*Above: Quilted patchwork of
batik fabric by Helen Bitar.*

*Right: Multicolored patch-
work wall hanging by Sally A.
Anderson.*

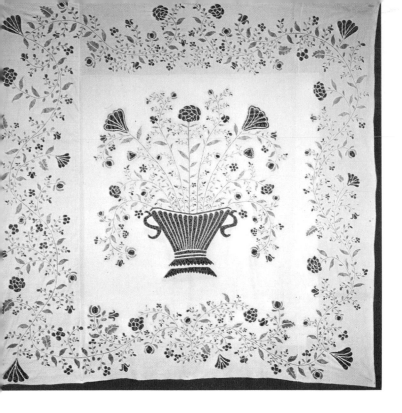

Above: Reverse appliqué quilt, possibly nineteenth century. Courtesy of the Shelburne Museum, Shelburne, Vermont

Above, right: Puff patchwork quilt by Helen Bitar. The padded patchwork squares are appliquéd and embroidered.

Right: The Liberty Rag Store *by Marilyn Pappas. Fabric collage with stitchery.*

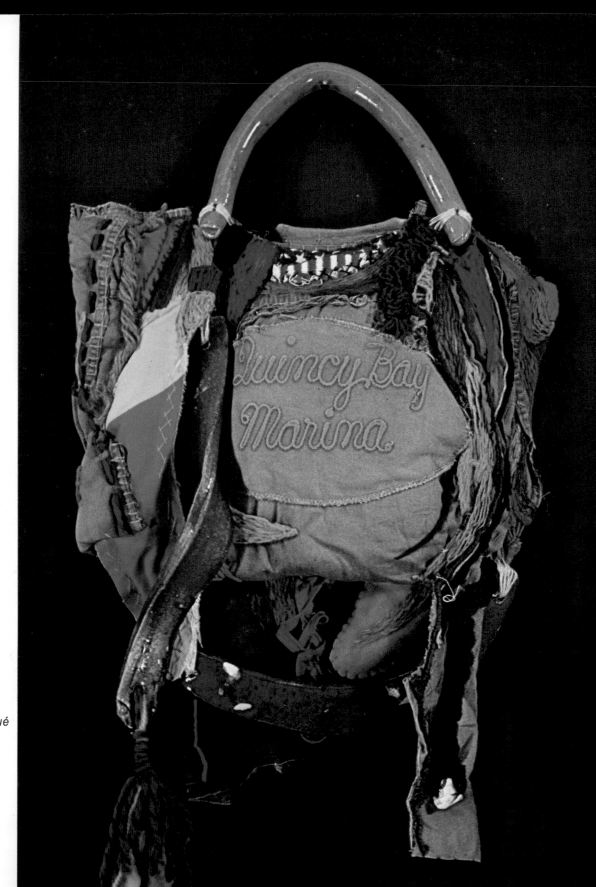

Bill's Bag by Marilyn Pappas. Fabric appliqué collage with stitchery and ceramic pieces.

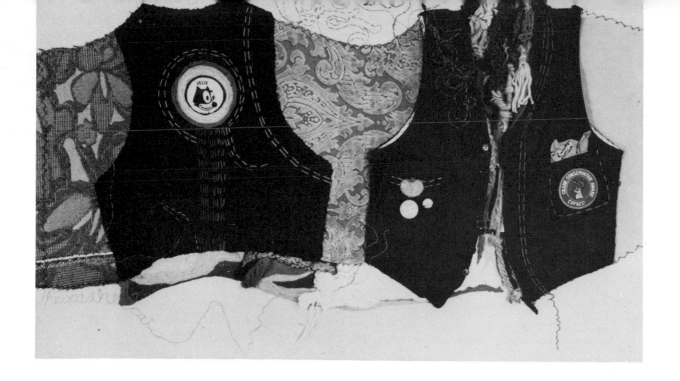

Pillow by Martha Miller. Machine-stitched, printed fabric collage.

Top: Felix the Cat *by Marilyn Pappas. Appliqué panel made of vests with velvet and brocade fabrics, assorted fibers, and other objects, on linen backing with stitchery. Photo Dave Read*

Left: Mrs. Burns *by Alma Lesch. Fabric collage portrait in black and white composed of an old cotton blouse, fan, hat pins, shoe buttons, and stitchery on linsey-woolsey.*

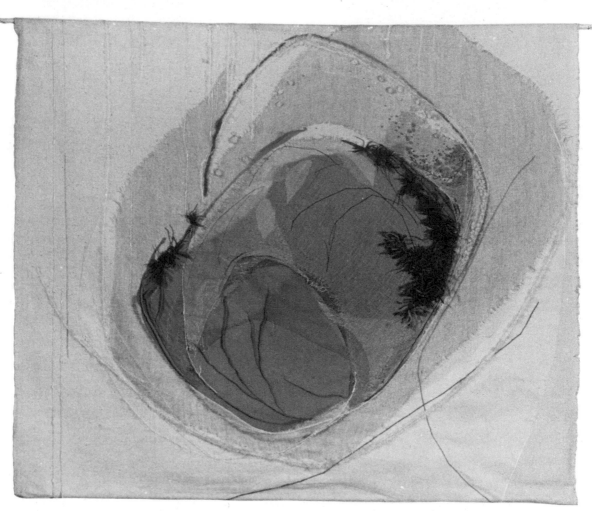

Fungus by Nancy Friedman. Wall hanging appliquéd with transparent fabrics and supplementary stitchery.

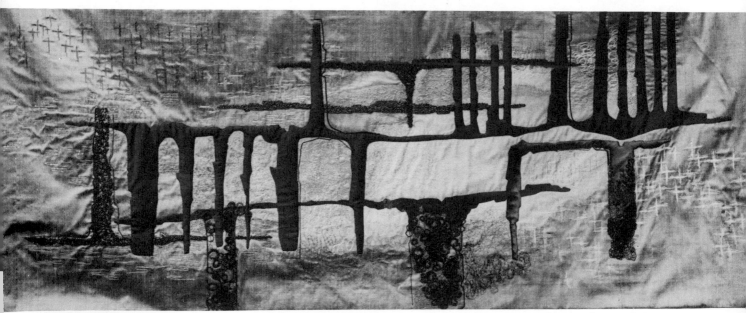

Advent altar frontal symbolizing the Passion by Beryl Dean. Shaded from purple to light turquoise, with superimposed shapes in black. Courtesy St. Margaret's Church, King's Lynn, Norfolk, England

Above, left and right: Details of a Parochet (Ark cloth) by Ina Golub. Appliqué of hand-woven silks with stitchery of wool, rayon, cotton, and metallic yarns, with crystal, pearl, and ceramic beads. Courtesy Temple Beth Ahm, Springfield, New Jersey. Photos Richard Kyle

Left: Waiting by Rozsika B. Blackstone. Machine-stitched multicolored felt appliqué. Photo Maurice Praga

Above: Organic Garden *by Sally A. Anderson. Machine-appliquéd soft sculpture, Dacron filled.*

Above, right: Burse *by Cynthia Kendzior. Bronze and gilt leather appliquéd on white ground.* Courtesy Church of the Holy Sepulchre, London, England

Right: Untitled appliqué by Andrea Smith. Stitched felt on burlap.

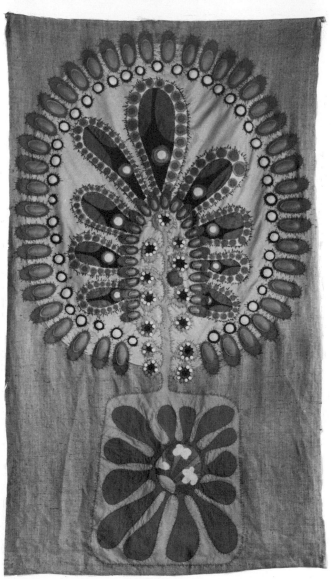

Above: Nine by Sally A. Anderson. Machine appliqué in close values of red.

Left: Winter Scene by Joan Kelly Russell. Appliqué of stitchery, transparent gauzes, and opaque fabrics.

Group of appliquéd costumes by Sas Colby

Above, right: Cape of brown velvet with silk hands and silk and satin motifs.

Above, left: Ruffle My Feathers, *a costume and mask of velvet and satin.*

Right: Geometrics, a cape in velvet Baby Block patchwork, with tinkling gold drops

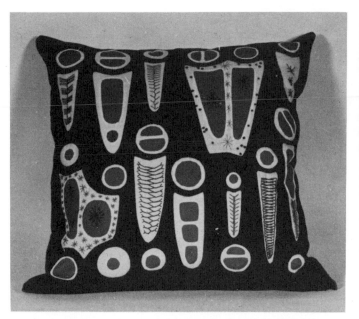

Reverse appliqué pillow in turquoise, olive green, and light blue, with olive green corduroy back by Hilda Kraus. Photo Yvette Klein

Above: Reverse appliqué pillow by Hilda Kraus. Red, white and blue broadcloth with red corduroy back and cotton floss stitchery. Photo Yvette Klein

Above, right: El Gato, reverse appliqué mola from the San Blas Islands. Collection Hanna Hale

Right: Mask by Norma Minkowitz. Cotton reverse appliqué and stitchery stretched over chicken wire. Photo K. Y. Fung

199

TO MAKE A MEDALLION RUG:

1. For each medallion select two contrasting colors of felt. Freely cut ovals or circles, one 6″ larger than the other.

2. Place the smaller medallion over the larger one. The large center area remains free of stitchery. Start machine stitching in widening concentric circles about 7″ in from the edge of the smaller circle. Each row of stitching is placed about the width of the presser foot away from the last row.

3. Cut pieces of yarn about 6″ long for fringe. Fold in half and assemble in groups of three. Slip the fold ½″ under the edge of the top layer of felt and machine stitch close to the edge, securing the top layer of felt, the folded edge of yarn, and the bottom layer of felt.

4. Slash medallions from the center, in irregular pie cuts, toward the first row of stitchery. Cut through both layers of felt.

5. Turn back both layers of felt over the stitchery to form rays around the open space in the center. Fasten the rays in place with one row of stitchery.

6. Arrange and place all finished medallions on an open-weave background fabric, such as burlap, monk's cloth, or Duraback. Machine-stitch in place.

7. Finish all open areas with hooking or turkeywork. Hooking usually requires stretching; turkeywork knotting with needle and thread does not. Add additional fringe of felt or yarn if desired.

(Design by Vesta Ward)

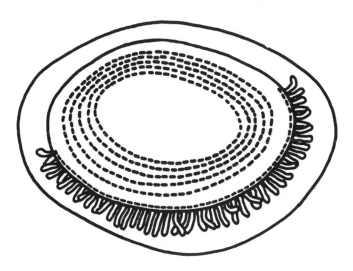

Medallion rug. Free stitchery of concentric circles, including the addition of cut yarn fringe.

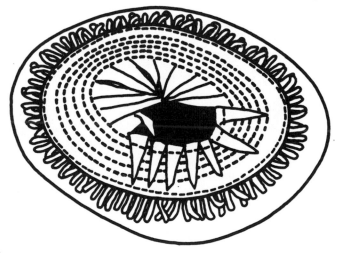

Slashing center area in pie-cut wedges. Fold back and stitch slashed edges, leaving center open space.

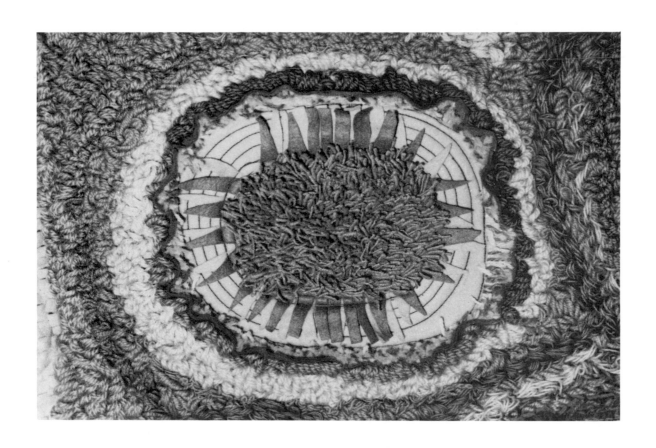

Medallion rug of felt, burlap, and wool in shades of rust, orange, gold, and silver designed by Vesta Ward. Above: Detail of medallion rug.

BIBLIOGRAPHY

EMBROIDERY

Christie, Mrs. Archibald. *Samplers and Stitches.* London: B. T. Batsford Ltd., 1920. Great Neck, New York: Hearthside Press, Inc., 1971

de Dillmont, Therese. *Encyclopedia of Needlework.* Mulhouse, France: D.M.C. Library

D'Harcourt, Raoul. *Textiles of Ancient Peru and Their Techniques.* Seattle: University of Washington Press, 1962

Fry, Gladys Windsor. *Embroidery and Needlework.* London: Sir Isaac Pitman & Sons, Ltd., 1959

Huish, Marcus. *Samplers and Tapestry Embroideries.* London: Longmans, Green & Co., 1913. New York: Dover Publications, 1970

Karasz, Mariska. *Adventure in Stitches.* New York: Funk & Wagnalls, Inc., 1959

The Story of Samplers. Philadelphia Museum of Art, 1971

Thomas, Mary. *Mary Thomas's Embroidery Book.* London: Hodder and Stoughton, 1935. New York: William Morrow & Company, Inc., 1936

Wardle, Patricia. *Guide to English Embroidery.* London: Victoria and Albert Museum, 1970

NEEDLEPOINT

Baker, Muriel L. *XYZ's of Canvas Embroidery.* Sturbridge, Massachusetts: Old Sturbridge Village, 1971

Hanley, Hope. *Needlepoint.* New York: Charles Scribner's Sons, 1964

Procter, Molly G. *Victorian Canvas Work: Berlin Woolwork.* New York: Drake Publishers, 1972. London: B. T. Batsford Ltd., 1972

Rhodes, Mary. *Ideas for Creative Embroidery.* Newton Centre, Massachusetts: Charles T. Branford Co., 1971. Published under the title *Ideas for Canvas Work.* London: B. T. Batsford Ltd., 1971

Snook, Barbara. *The Craft of Florentine Embroidery.* New York: Charles Scribner's Sons, 1971

Springall, Diana. *Canvas Embroidery.* Newton Centre, Massachusetts: Charles T. Branford Co., 1969. London: B. T. Batsford Ltd., 1971

PATCHWORK AND QUILTING

Colby, Averil. *Quilting.* New York: Charles Scribner's Sons, 1971. London: B. T. Batsford Ltd., 1972

Finley, Ruth E. *Old Patchwork Quilts.* Newton Centre, Massachusetts: Charles T. Branford Co., 1929

Green, Sylvia. *Patchwork for Beginners.* London: Studio Vista, 1971

Notes on Applied Work and Patchwork. London: Victoria and Albert Museum, 1938

Icarus *by Norma Minkowitz. Appliqué of machine stitchery and closely crocheted ruffles on a burlap background, padded with Dacron floss and backed with velvet. Collection Mr. and Mrs. Howard Kurt. Photo K. Y. Fung*

INDEX